The Italian Vegan

The Italian Vegan

Georgina Ferrari

ATHENA PRESS
LONDON

THE ITALIAN VEGAN
Copyright © Georgina Ferrari 2008

ISBN: 978 1 84748 327 0

First published 2008
ATHENA PRESS
Queen's House, 2 Holly Road
Twickenham TW1 4EG
United Kingdom

Printed for Athena Press

For all vegans – and non

*Special thanks go to my sister, Rosetta,
who jogged my memory and whose
computer skills I could not have done without.*

*Special prayers go to my mother
and my mother-in-law,
who taught me so much.*

Foreword

The following recipes have been chosen after years of being a vegan living in Italy.

Each one is based on authentic peasant dishes and personal experience, and are by their very nature meat and animal-product free. They are simple, but delicious – the real taste of Italy.

The salt used in the recipes should be fine-ground sea salt, unless specified.

The recipes are all for about four or five people, depending on appetites, of course!

ESSENTIAL KITCHEN EQUIPMENT

Make sure you have the following in your kitchen:

- ✓ At least one very large heavy-bottomed frying pan, ideally about 40cm in diameter
- ✓ A very large heavy-bottomed saucepan, again about 40cm in diameter
- ✓ A large work surface (e.g. kitchen table)
- ✓ Plenty of large mixing bowls
- ✓ Large serving bowls and dishes
- ✓ Large heavy oven trays and dishes

RECIPES

———◦◯◦———

SOUPS

PASTA

RICE

POLENTA, GNOCCHI AND BARLEY

PIZZAS, PIES AND SNACKS

VEGETABLES

SALADS

SWEETS

PRESERVES

SOUPS

COURGETTE FLOWER SOUP

Ciambotta

300g courgettes

200g courgette flowers

500g potatoes

1 small onion

50ml Italian extra-virgin olive oil

2tsp salt

1. Remove and discard the pistils from the courgette flowers and wash well
2. Wash and dice the courgettes
3. Peel and dice the potatoes
4. Peel and finely chop the onion
5. Put 1lt water and the oil into a saucepan and add the vegetables
6. Bring to the boil and add 2tsp salt
7. Reduce to a simmer and allow to cook gently for 1½–2 hours, stirring occasionally
8. Serve very hot with dry toast

Courgette flowers can be hard to find in the shops, so perhaps, on special request, you could find a gardener willing to give up his springtime flowers for this delightful, delicate soup. They do freeze well.

COURGETTE SOUP

Minestra di Zucchine

1kg courgettes

2 large potatoes

1 400g can chopped tomatoes

1 small onion

1½ lt vegetable stock

50ml Italian extra-virgin olive oil

200g small pasta shells (conchigliette) – or other small pasta

1tsp chopped parsley

Grated nutmeg to taste

1tsp salt

---

1. Peel and finely chop the onion
2. Wash and dice the courgettes
3. Peel and dice the potatoes
4. In a large heavy-bottomed saucepan, soften the onion in the olive oil for a few minutes without browning
5. Add the tomatoes, potato and courgettes and stir well
7. Add the salt and cook over a gentle heat for about 15 minutes, stirring frequently
8. Add the hot stock and continue cooking for another 15 minutes
9. Add the pasta shells and cook for 12–15 minutes, stirring frequently
10. Taste for salt, adding if necessary, and stir well
11. Before serving, sprinkle with the chopped parsley and a little grated nutmeg

FARMHOUSE SOUP

Zuppa del Casale

> *300g spelt (farro)*
>
> *300g dried white haricot beans*
>
> *1 garlic clove*
>
> *3 leaves fresh sage*
>
> *1 sprig fresh rosemary*
>
> *1 small onion*
>
> *500ml vegetable stock*
>
> *50ml Italian extra-virgin olive oil*
>
> *1tsp salt*
>
> *Black pepper to taste*

1. Soak the haricot beans in cold water overnight
2. Peel and slit the garlic clove lengthways but leave it whole
3. Chop the sage leaves
4. Detach the rosemary needles from the branch and chop
5. In a saucepan, boil the beans in about 1lt unsalted water together with the garlic clove, chopped rosemary and sage for roughly 2 hours until the beans are soft
6. When the beans are cooked, remove and discard the garlic clove
7. Pass the beans and herbs, together with any cooking liquid there is, through a vegetable mill or food processor and reduce to a paste
8. Peel and finely chop the onion
9. In a large heavy-bottomed saucepan, soften the onion in the olive oil for a few minutes without browning
10. Add the spelt and stock and cook for about 10 minutes, stirring occasionally

11. Add the mashed beans and salt and continue cooking for another 30–40 minutes, stirring frequently; if necessary, top up with more hot water

12. When the spelt is cooked, check for taste, adding a little salt if necessary

13. Give a final stir and add a dash of black pepper

14. Leave to stand for about 5 minutes before serving

This is an ancient dish, typical of the Garfagnana area of Tuscany.

GRANDMA'S SOUP

Minestra della Nonna

100g Italian carnaroli or ribe rice

1 large leek

150g fresh spinach

1 large potato

1lt strong vegetable stock

100ml crushed tomato (passata)

50ml corn oil

---

1. Wash the spinach leaves well and shred
2. Wash the leek well and slice into rings
3. In very large heavy-bottomed saucepan, fry the leek rings in the corn oil for a few minutes without browning
4. Add the shredded spinach and sauté for a few minutes
5. Add the stock and return to the boil
6. Peel and dice the potato
7. Add the potato and the crushed tomato to the saucepan
8. Cook through gently for about 30 minutes
9. Add the rice and cook for about another 15–20 minutes, stirring frequently
10. Serve very hot with crusty bread

This is perfect on a cold winter's day with a good hearty red wine to accompany it.

MINESTRONE

150g frozen beans (or 300g fresh) (Italian borlotti are best)

150g frozen peas (or 300g fresh)

150g carrots

150g French green beans

150g leeks

200g courgettes

200g potatoes

100g celery

1 small onion

1 400g tin peeled tomatoes

1tsp chopped parsley

1tsp chopped basil

Approx 25ml Italian extra-virgin olive oil

150g short pasta (ditaloni)

3tsp salt

Black pepper to taste

1. Wash and finely slice the celery, leeks, courgettes and carrots
2. Peel and finely slice the onion
3. Top and tail the green beans, wash well and cut into 3cm pieces
4. If using fresh beans and peas, shell these
5. Put all the vegetables (excluding the potatoes) and the tinned tomatoes into a very large saucepan with about 1½lt water and bring to the boil
6. Allow to simmer for about 2 hours with a lid
7. Peel and cut the potatoes into small cubes and add to the saucepan, along with the salt and basil and parsley

8. Continue cooking for about another 20 minutes
9. Add the pasta and cook for about 10–12 minutes, stirring occasionally
10. When the pasta is cooked, taste for salt and stir well
11. Add a tablespoon of oil at the very end, together with a dash of black pepper
12. Allow to cool slightly before serving

PASTINA STARS IN VEGETABLE BROTH

Stelline in Brodo Vegetale

---

2 carrots

1 stick celery

1 onion

1 courgette

1 potato

2 tomatoes (fresh or tinned)

3 sprigs parsley

3tsp salt

300g small pasta stars

Italian extra-virgin olive oil

---

1. Peel and roughly chop the carrots, onion and potato
2. Wash the celery, courgette, parsley and tomatoes well and roughly chop
3. Put all the chopped vegetables into a saucepan with 2lt cold water, add salt and bring to the boil, then reduce the heat and allow to simmer for 2 hours
4. Strain the broth and discard the vegetables
5. Return the broth to the saucepan and bring to a fast boil, and add the pasta stars
6. Cook for about 10 minutes, stirring frequently
7. Add salt to taste
8. Serve immediately with a drizzle of olive oil on each plate

This is a firm favourite among young children in Italy, but also their parents!

PULSE SOUP

Zuppa di Legumi

150g dried white haricot beans

250g frozen peas

150g dried Italian borlotti beans

150g dried chickpeas

1 carrot

1 small onion

1 stick celery

2tsp concentrated tomato paste

50ml Italian extra-virgin olive oil

1tsp chopped parsley

1tsp dried marjoram

2–3tsp salt

---

1. Soak the haricot beans, borlotti beans and chickpeas together in a bowl of cold water overnight
2. Peel the carrot and the onion and chop very finely
3. Wash the celery and slice as thinly as possible
4. In a large heavy-bottomed saucepan, soften the onion, carrot and celery in the olive oil for a few minutes
5. Drain the beans and chickpeas and add these to the saucepan
6. Add the peas and fry for a few minutes, stirring frequently
7. Add 1½lt water and bring to the boil
8. Lower the heat and allow to cook gently with a lid for at least 2 hours, stirring occasionally

9. Dissolve the tomato paste in a little water and add this to the soup

10. Add chopped parsley and marjoram

11. Cook through for another 30 minutes and check to see if the beans are cooked

12. Finally, add salt and stir well

13. Serve the soup with slices of toast – piping hot

PUMPKIN SOUP

Zuppa di Zucca

---

1 pumpkin, about 1kg in weight

1 small onion

50ml olive oil (not extra-virgin)

1 bay leaf

2tsp salt

Black pepper to taste

---

1. Peel and core the pumpkin, retaining only the orange flesh
2. Cut the pulp up into large chunks
3. Peel and finely slice the onion
4. In a large heavy-bottomed saucepan, soften the onion in the olive oil without browning
5. Add the chunks of pumpkin and fry for a few minutes, stirring frequently
6. Add salt, about 1½lt cold water and the bay leaf
7. Stir well and bring to the boil
8. Reduce the heat and allow to simmer with a lid for about 2 hours, stirring occasionally
9. Remove and discard the bay leaf
10. Pass the soup in a blender or a vegetable mill
11. Taste for salt, adding some if necessary
12. Serve piping hot with a dash of freshly milled black pepper and with fresh crusty bread

PASTA

'ANGRY' PASTA QUILLS

Penne all'Arrabbiata

> 400g pasta quills
>
> 2 garlic gloves
>
> 1 small onion
>
> 3 whole red chillies
>
> 1 400g can chopped tomatoes
>
> 50ml Italian extra-virgin olive oil
>
> 5tsp salt

1. Peel and finely chop the onion and crush the chillies
2. Peel the garlic cloves and slit them lengthways, leaving them whole
3. In a very large heavy-bottomed frying pan, fry the onions, crushed chillies and garlic in the olive oil for a few minutes, but do not brown
4. Add the chopped tomatoes, along with 400ml water and 1tsp salt and cook through on a slow heat for about 1 hour
5. Remove the garlic cloves and discard
6. In a large saucepan, boil 3lt water and add 4tsp salt
7. When the water is boiling, throw in the pasta quills and stir
8. Cook on a fierce heat for about 12 minutes, stirring occasionally
9. Check to see if the pasta is *al dente* (slightly undercooked) and then drain
10. Throw the pasta into the frying pan with the sauce and over a fierce heat, fry for a minute, stirring frequently
11. Serve immediately

If you want it 'angrier', add another two or three chillies.

BOWTIE PASTA WITH COURGETTES

Farfalle alle Zucchine

1kg courgettes

1 small onion

100ml Italian extra-virgin olive oil

400g bowtie pasta (farfalle)

6tsp salt

Black pepper to taste

---

1. Wash the courgettes and slice into very thin discs, preferably with an electric slicer

2. Peel the onion and slice very thinly

3. In a very large heavy-bottomed saucepan, soften the onion in the olive oil for a few minutes

4. Add the courgette discs and 2tsp salt and fry on a high heat for a few minutes, stirring frequently

5. Lower the heat and partially cover

6. Cook the courgettes gently for about 2 hours, stirring occasionally

7. After this time, give the courgette mixture a good stir – it should be quite pulpy

8. In a separate large saucepan, bring 3lt water to the boil, with 4tsp salt, throw in the pasta and cook for about 12–15 minutes, stirring frequently

11. Drain the pasta well and add to the saucepan with the courgette mixture

12. Stir very well and serve with freshly milled black pepper

CHESTNUT TAGLIATELLE

Tagliatelle con Farina di Castagne

> *300g chestnut flour*
> *200g plain flour*
> *50g polenta (cornmeal)*
> *4tsp salt*
> *50ml olive oil (not extra-virgin)*
> *100g roughly chopped walnuts*
> *Extra flour for dusting*

1. Put the chestnut flour and the white flour into a large bowl and mix
2. Gradually add cold water until you have a compact, smooth dough that is not sticky
3. Dust a large work surface liberally with flour
4. Roll out the dough to a thickness of about 2mm, to form a large rectangle
5. Sprinkle over with the polenta flour
6. Allow to dry for about 1 hour
7. In the meantime, prepare 3 large trays with clean, dry tea towels and dust with flour
8. Roll up the pastry like a Swiss roll
9. With a very sharp knife, cut the roll into approx ½cm thick slices
10. Unravel the slices to get thin tagliatelle
11. Lay these out onto the floured trays
12. When all the tagliatelle are made, cover with a clean tea towel and leave aside to dry out completely in a cool, dry place (not the fridge) for 24 hours

13. Add the salt to 3lt water and bring to the boil
14. Throw in the tagliatelle and cook for about 15–20 minutes, stirring frequently
15. In a very large frying pan, heat the chopped walnuts for a few seconds in the olive oil
16. Drain the tagliatelle well and add to the frying pan with the walnuts
17. Toss well and serve

These tagliatelle are a real taste of the days when people lived remotely in wild mountain woods in the north of Italy.

LIGURIAN TROFIE

Trofie alla Ligure

> 400g plain flour
>
> 300g French green beans
>
> 500g potatoes
>
> Several handfuls fresh basil leaves
>
> 50g pine nuts
>
> 1 garlic clove
>
> ½tsp coarse salt
>
> 75ml Italian extra-virgin olive oil
>
> 4tsp salt
>
> Extra flour for dusting

1. Sift the flour into a large bowl
2. Gradually add cold water until you have a firm dough
3. With well-floured hands, knead the dough until it is smooth and no longer sticky
4. On two large trays, lay out two clean, dry tea towels and dust them with flour
5. Roll the dough out to a thickness of about 2mm
6. Cut into small strips, approx 2cm x ½cm
7. With well-floured fingers, give each strip a few twists
8. Place each trofia, or twist, onto the floured tea towels, ensuring that they do not touch each other
9. Cover the trays of trofie with a clean, dry tea towel and leave in a cool, dry place (not the fridge) for at least 3 hours, preferably overnight, until they have dried out

10. Top and tail the French beans, wash well and cut into pieces of about 2cm

11. Peel and dice the potatoes

12. Wash the basil leaves well

13. Peel the garlic clove

14. Put the basil leaves, the pine nuts, the garlic clove, the coarse salt, and 50ml olive oil into a food processor and blend to a fine paste

15. In a large saucepan, boil 3lt water with salt

16. Throw in the beans and potatoes and cook on a rolling boil for about 10 minutes

17. Add the trofie pasta to the saucepan and continue cooking for about 12–15 minutes, stirring frequently, until cooked

18. Drain the pasta and vegetables and return to the saucepan

19. Add the remaining 25ml olive oil and the basil paste and stir well

20. Transfer to a large dish and serve

These 'trofie' are long and laborious to make, but if you get together perhaps with friends or members of the family, it can become fun. If you have a pasta machine, this can be made easier by making the strips using the tagliatelle blades and then cutting them up. They can be made in advance, and you can make a large quantity and freeze them in batches. Alternatively, you might find them ready-made in Italian delicatessens!

ORECCHIETTE WITH TURNIP TOPS

Orecchiette alle Cime di Rapa

2kg turnip tops (if these are difficult to find, use small broccoli heads)

3 garlic cloves

100ml Italian extra-virgin olive oil

400g orecchiette pasta

6tsp salt

---

1. Pick the small leaves and the unopened florets off the stalks of the turnip tops and put into a bowl, discarding any very large or discoloured leaves

2. Wash and roughly chop the turnip tops

3. Peel and slit the garlic cloves lengthways, leaving them whole

4. In a very large, heavy-bottomed frying pan, fry the garlic in the oil for a few minutes

5. Add the turnip tops and 2tsp salt and stir well

6. Cook the turnip tops over a moderate heat for about 1 hour, until they have diminished in volume

7. Continue cooking until very little water is left, and they begin to fry

8. Remove and discard the garlic cloves

9. Boil about 3lt water with 4tsp salt in a large saucepan, add the *orecchiette* and cook for about 15 minutes

10. Drain the *orecchiette* well and immediately add to the frying pan with the turnip tops

11. Fry for a few seconds, stirring frequently, and serve immediately

ORECCHIETTE WITH LENTILS

Orecchiette con le Lenticchie

400g tinned lentils or 200g dried lentils

2 large onions

75ml Italian extra-virgin olive oil

2 chilli peppers

5–6tsp salt

400g orecchiette pasta

1. If using dried lentils, soak overnight and then cook in unsalted water for about 2 hours until soft and then add 1tsp salt

2. Peel and slice the onions into very fine rings

3. Put the oil in a very large heavy-bottom frying pan and gently soften the onions; cover with a lid and allow to sweat for about 20 minutes until soft

4. Add the drained lentils, crushed chilli peppers and 1tsp salt, and stir well

5. In a large saucepan add 4tsp salt to 3lt water and bring to the boil

6. Add the *orecchiette* and cook for 15 minutes, stirring occasionally

7. Drain the pasta well and immediately transfer to the frying pan with the lentils

8. Stir well over a high flame for about 2 minutes

9. Check for seasoning and serve

PASTA AND BEANS

Pasta e Fagioli

300g dried small haricot beans

1 small onion

1 garlic clove

50ml Italian extra-virgin olive oil

300g ditaloni pasta (or any other short pasta)

1tsp dried marjoram

1tsp chopped parsley

1tsp concentrated tomato paste

2tsp salt

---

1. Soak the beans in cold water for at least 4 hours, preferably overnight
2. Peel and finely chop the onion
3. Peel and slit the garlic clove lengthways, leaving it whole
4. In a large heavy-bottomed saucepan, soften the onion and the garlic in the olive oil for a few minutes without browning
5. Remove the garlic clove and discard
6. Add the drained haricot beans and fry for a few minutes, stirring frequently
7. Add 1½lt cold water, the marjoram, the parsley and the concentrated tomato paste and bring to the boil
8. Lower the heat, cover and allow to simmer for about 2–3 hours until the beans are soft
9. Add salt and return to the boil
10. Add the pasta and cook for about 20 minutes, stirring frequently, until there is very little liquid left

11. Check for salt, adding if necessary

12. Leave aside for a few minutes before serving

Another southern Italian classic, often further enriched by drizzling a little extra-virgin olive oil over each plate before serving.

PASTA AND CHICKPEAS

Pasta e Ceci

300g dried chickpeas

1 small onion

1 garlic clove

1 small carrot

1 small stick celery

50ml Italian extra-virgin olive oil

300g ditaloni pasta (or any other short pasta)

2tsp salt

1tsp chopped parsley

---

1. Soak the chickpeas in cold water overnight
2. Drain them and then boil in unsalted water for about 2–3 hours until they soften
3. Peel the onion and carrot and chop as finely as possible
4. Wash the celery stick and slice very finely
5. Peel the garlic clove and slit, but leave whole
6. In a large heavy-bottomed saucepan, soften the onion, carrot, celery and garlic in the olive oil for a few minutes without browning
7. Drain and add the chickpeas to the saucepan and sauté for a few minutes
8. Add 1lt water and bring to the boil
9. Lower the heat and allow to cook gently for about 1 hour with a lid, stirring occasionally
10. Remove and discard the garlic clove
11. Add the pasta and salt and stir well

12. Cook for about 15–20 minutes, stirring frequently until the pasta is cooked

13. Check for salt, adding if necessary

14. Add the chopped parsley and serve

PASTA AND PEAS

Pasta e Piselli

400g frozen peas

1 small onion

1 small carrot

1 garlic clove

50ml extra-virgin olive oil

2tsp salt

Black pepper to taste

1tsp chopped parsley

300g short pasta (ditaloni)

---

1. Peel and finely chop the onion and carrot
2. Peel and slit the garlic clove lengthways, leaving it whole
3. Heat the oil in a large saucepan and add the onions, garlic clove and carrots; cover with a lid and allow to gently sweat
4. Add the frozen peas and fry for a few minutes, stirring frequently
5. Add 1lt water and bring to the boil, then lower the heat and allow to simmer for about one hour
6. Remove and discard the garlic clove
7. Add salt
8. Raise the heat and add the pasta and cook for about 20 minutes, stirring occasionally
9. Taste for salt, then just before serving add the chopped parsley and give a final stir

PASTA SHELLS WITH BROAD BEANS

Pasta e Fave

> 1kg fresh broad beans (or 500g ready-shelled frozen beans)
>
> 1 large carrot
>
> 1 stick celery
>
> 1 small onion
>
> 1 garlic glove
>
> 50ml Italian extra-virgin olive oil
>
> 300g pasta shells
>
> 2tsp salt

1. Peel and finely chop the carrot and onion
2. Wash and finely chop the celery stick
3. Peel and slit the garlic clove lengthways, leaving it whole
4. Shell the broad beans, if using fresh
5. In a heavy-bottomed saucepan, soften the onion, carrot, celery and garlic in the olive oil for a few minutes
6. Add the broad beans and fry for a few minutes, stirring frequently
7. Add 1½lt water and bring to the boil
8. Reduce the heat, cover and allow to cook gently for about 2 hours
9. Remove and discard the garlic clove
10. Add salt
11. Raise the heat and add the pasta shells
12. Cook for about 20 minutes, stirring very frequently, until the pasta is cooked
13. Check for salt, adding if necessary and serve

PASTA SHELLS WITH POTATOES

Pasta e Patate

> *1kg potatoes*
>
> *2 garlic cloves*
>
> *1 small onion*
>
> *1tsp chopped parsley*
>
> *300g pasta shells*
>
> *50ml Italian extra-virgin olive oil*
>
> *2tsp salt*

1. Peel and dice the potatoes
2. Peel the garlic cloves and slit them lengthways, leaving them whole
3. Peel and finely chop the onion
4. In a large heavy-bottomed saucepan, soften the onion and garlic in the olive oil for a few minutes without browning
5. Remove and discard the garlic cloves
6. Add the diced potato and fry for a few minutes
7. Add 1½lt water, the chopped parsley and salt
8. Bring to the boil, lower the heat and simmer for about 1 hour, stirring frequently
9. Return to the boil and throw in the pasta shells
10. Cook through for about 15 minutes, stirring frequently until most of the water has evaporated
11. Taste for salt and leave to stand for a few minutes before serving

PASTA WITH AUBERGINE SAUCE

Pasta con Sugo alle Melanzane

> *500g dark, plump aubergines*
>
> *1 small onion*
>
> *1 garlic clove*
>
> *50ml Italian extra-virgin olive oil*
>
> *1 400g can chopped tomatoes*
>
> *2 leaves fresh basil*
>
> *400g tortiglioni pasta (or other large pasta shapes)*
>
> *5tsp salt*

1. Wash the aubergines well and dice
2. Peel and finely chop the onion
3. Peel and slit the garlic clove lengthways, leaving it whole
4. In a large heavy-bottomed frying pan, soften the onion and garlic in the olive oil for a few minutes without browning
5. Add the diced aubergines together with 1tsp salt and fry for a few minutes, stirring frequently
6. Lower the heat and cook gently for about 30 minutes, stirring occasionally
7. Add the tomatoes, with 400ml water and the basil leaves, and cook through for about 2 hours, stirring occasionally, until there is very little water left
9. Remove and discard the garlic clove
10. Taste for salt, adding a little if necessary
11. In a large saucepan, add 4tsp salt to 3lt water and bring to the boil
12. Throw in the *tortiglioni* and cook for 12–15 minutes, stirring frequently
13. Drain the pasta well and add to the aubergine sauce
14. Mix well and serve

PASTA WITH FRESH TOMATO

Pasta con Pomodoro Fresco

500g fresh ripe tomatoes

5 leaves fresh basil

50ml Italian extra-virgin olive oil

400g fusilli pasta

5tsp salt

---

1. Wash and dice the tomatoes
2. Chop the basil leaves
3. Place the tomatoes and the basil in a large bowl with 1tsp salt and the olive oil, mix well and let stand for about 1 hour
4. In a large saucepan, add 4tsp salt to 3lt water and bring to the boil
6. Throw in the fusilli and cook for 12–15 minutes, stirring frequently
7. Drain the pasta and add to the bowl of fresh tomatoes
8. Mix well and serve

This pasta can also been eaten cold but, if so, the pasta should be cooked for no more than 10 minutes.

SPAGHETTI WITH FRIED BREAD

Spaghetti con la Mollica

> *3 garlic cloves*
> *200ml Italian extra-virgin olive oil*
> *100g breadcrumbs*
> *400g spaghetti*
> *4tsp salt*

1. Add the salt to 3lt water and bring to the boil

2. Add the spaghetti and cook for about 10–15 minutes, stirring frequently

3. In the meantime, peel the garlic cloves and slit them lengthways, leaving them whole

4. Heat the oil in a very large frying pan

5. Fry the garlic in the oil for a few minutes until it begins to brown, then remove and discard

6. When the spaghetti is *al dente* (slightly undercooked), drain well and immediately add to the frying pan with the oil

7. Add the breadcrumbs to the spaghetti and stir well over a high heat for about 5 minutes

8. Serve immediately

This a very old poor-man's recipe, from the remote areas of Sicily. It is simple but extremely good!

SPAGHETTI WITH GARLIC, OIL AND CHILLI PEPPER

Spaghetti all'Aglio, Olio e Peperoncino

150ml Italian extra-virgin olive oil

3 chilli peppers

6 garlic cloves

400g spaghetti

4tsp salt

1. Peel the garlic cloves and slit them lengthways, leaving them whole
2. Crush the chilli peppers
3. In a very large heavy-bottomed frying pan, soften the garlic cloves and the chilli peppers in the olive oil for a few minutes without browning
4. Remove from the heat
5. In a separate saucepan, add the salt to 3lt water and bring to the boil
6. Throw the spaghetti into the boiling water and boil over a fierce heat for about 12–15 minutes, stirring frequently, until the spaghetti is just *al dente* (slightly undercooked)
7. Drain the spaghetti well and immediately add to the frying pan with the oil
8. Fry the spaghetti in the oil over a high flame for a minute or two, stirring frequently
9. Serve immediately

This is a great emergency dish if unexpected guests turn up – and always very popular.

SPAGHETTI WITH PESTO SAUCE

Spaghetti al Pesto

Several handfuls fresh basil leaves

50g pine nuts

50ml Italian extra-virgin olive oil

½ tsp coarse salt

1 garlic clove

400g spaghetti (or ideally, trenette)

4 tsp salt

1. Wash the basil leaves
2. Peel the garlic clove
3. Put the basil leaves, pine nuts, garlic clove, coarse salt and oil together in a food processor and blend to a fine paste
4. Add the salt to 3lt water and bring to the boil
5. When the water is boiling, throw in the spaghetti and cook for about 12–15 minutes, stirring occasionally
6. Drain the spaghetti well and coat with the pesto sauce, adding olive oil as necessary
7. Serve immediately

Traditionally, *trenette* (a sort of flat spaghetti) are served with pesto sauce.

SPAGHETTI WITH TOMATO SAUCE

Spaghetti al Pomodoro

> ½ small onion
>
> 1 garlic clove
>
> 50ml Italian extra-virgin olive oil
>
> 1 400g can chopped tomatoes
>
> 2 small basil leaves
>
> 400g spaghetti
>
> 5tsp salt

1. Peel and very finely slice the onion
2. Peel and slit the garlic clove lengthways, leaving it whole
3. Soften the onion and garlic in the oil for a few minutes, without browning
4. Add the tomatoes, 1tsp salt, the basil leaves and 400ml water and bring to the boil
5. Lower the heat and allow to very gently simmer for 3 hours, stirring occasionally
7. Remove the garlic clove and discard
8. In a large saucepan, add 4tsp salt to 3lt water and bring to the boil
9. When the water boils, throw in the spaghetti and cook for 12–15 minutes
10. Drain the spaghetti well and return to the saucepan
11. Add the tomato sauce and coat the spaghetti well
12. Serve immediately

This is a southern Italian classic – no true southern Italian could live without!

SPINACH TAGLIATELLE

Tagliatelle Verdi

300g plain flour

500g fresh spinach

25g semolina

50ml Italian extra-virgin olive oil

4tsp salt

Black pepper to taste

Extra flour for dusting

---

1. Wash the spinach very well and place in a large saucepan over a moderate heat

2. Allow the spinach to cook without any water (it will form its own liquid) for about 30 minutes, stirring occasionally, then drain well and chop as finely as possible – preferably in a food processor

3. In a large bowl, place the flour and make a well in the centre

4. Add the chopped spinach and a little cold water – a little at a time

5. Using your hands, mix well to form a compact dough

6. Generously dust a work surface with flour and roll out the dough to a thickness of about 2mm and form a large rectangle

7. Sprinkle the semolina all over the sheet of dough

8. Prepare three large trays with clean, dry tea towels on them and dust generously with flour

9. Roll up the dough like a Swiss roll

10. Using a sharp knife, cut through the roll at a thickness of about ½cm

11. Unravel each slice to form tagliatelle

12. Place each tagliatella onto the floured trays, ensuring they do not touch each other

13. When all the tagliatelle are made, cover the trays with other clean, dry tea towels and leave aside in a cool, dry place (not the fridge) for at least 3 hours – preferably overnight

14. Add the salt to 3lt water and bring to the boil

15. Throw in the tagliatelle and cook for about 12–15 minutes, stirring frequently

16. Drain well and add the olive oil

17. Serve immediately with a dash of freshly milled black pepper

'STRANGLE THE PRIESTS!' PASTA

Strozzapreti

400g plain flour

50ml Italian extra-virgin olive oil

1 small onion

1 garlic glove

1 400g can chopped tomatoes

3 leaves fresh basil

5tsp salt

Extra flour for dusting

---

1. Put the flour into a large bowl and gradually add cold water until you have a firm dough
2. Knead the dough until it is smooth and no longer sticky
3. Dust a large work surface generously with flour
4. Roll out the dough to a thickness of about 2mm, dusting with flour frequently
5. Prepare several trays with clean tea towels, dusted with flour
6. Cut the rolled out dough into strips of about 1cm x 4cm
7. With well-floured fingers, give each little strip one twist and lay out onto the floured trays
8. Continue forming little *strozzapreti* until all the dough is used up
9. Cover the trays with clean, dry tea towels and leave in a cool place to dry out (not the fridge) – preferably overnight
10. Peel and slit the garlic clove lengthways, leaving it whole
11. Peel and very finely chop the onion
12. In a heavy-bottomed saucepan, soften the chopped onion and the garlic in the olive oil for a few minutes without browning

13. Add the chopped tomatoes and 400ml water, together with the basil leaves and 1tsp salt

14. Bring to the boil, then lower the heat and allow to cook through for at least 2 hours, stirring occasionally

15. Remove and discard the garlic clove

16. In a large saucepan add 4tsp salt to 3lt water and bring to the boil

17. Throw in the *strozzapreti*, and cook for about 12–15 minutes, stirring frequently

18. Drain well, return to the saucepan and coat with the tomato sauce

19. Serve immediately

Home-made pasta is long and laborious to make, but the taste is fabulous – so well worth the effort.

The theory surrounding the name – 'Strangle the Priests! – is said to come from the days when the Church had power over the peasants. They saw the twisting of these little pieces of pasta as a sort of 'death wish' on the priests as they 'strangled' each piece!

SUNDAY TAGLIATELLE WITH BEAN SAUCE

Tagliatelle della Domenica con Sugo di Fagioli

> *400g plain flour*
>
> *25g semolina*
>
> *1 small onion*
>
> *200g dried white haricot beans*
>
> *1 garlic clove*
>
> *50ml Italian extra-virgin olive oil*
>
> *1 400g can chopped tomatoes*
>
> *5tsp salt*
>
> *Extra flour for dusting*

1. Place the flour into a bowl and gradually add cold water until you have a firm dough

2. Roll the dough out to a thickness of about 2mm on a well-floured work surface and form a large rectangle

3. Sprinkle the rolled out dough with a little semolina and allow to stand for about 1 hour

4. Prepare three large trays with clean, dry tea towels dusted with flour

5. Very carefully roll up the dough, like a Swiss roll

6. Using a sharp knife, cut through the roll at a thickness of about ½cm

7. Lay out the tagliatelle on the floured trays, taking care not to let them touch each other

8. Cover each tray with another clean, dry tea towel and leave in a cool, dry place (not the fridge) to dry out for several hours – preferably overnight

9. Put the beans into a bowl of unsalted cold water and leave to soak overnight

10. The next day, boil the beans in 1lt unsalted water for 2 hours

11. Peel and finely slice the onion

12. Peel and slit the garlic clove lengthways, leaving it whole

13. In a heavy-bottomed saucepan, soften the onion and garlic in the olive oil without browning

14. Add the chopped tomatoes and 1tsp salt and stir

15. Add the beans together with their cooking liquid

16. Cook the sauce for about 2 hours over a gentle heat, stirring occasionally

17. When the sauce is cooked, remove and discard the garlic clove

18. Taste for salt, adding a little if necessary

19. In a large saucepan, add 4tsp salt to 3lt water and bring to the boil

20. Throw in the tagliatelle and cook for 12–15 minutes, stirring very frequently

21. Drain the tagliatelle and add to the bean and tomato sauce. Stir well

22. Serve immediately

These are hard work to make, but well worth it. They can be made more easily if you are lucky enough to have a pasta machine.

These are (or rather, were) a typical special Sunday or Feast Day (Christmas, Easter or other such festivities) pasta dish in the south of Italy – all the women of the family would work together the day before making the tagliatelle. It was seen as a way of showing love and affection for the family.

'WHORE'S' SPAGHETTI

Spaghetti alla Puttanesca

> 1 400g can peeled tomatoes
>
> 50ml Italian extra-virgin olive oil
>
> 100g whole olives (preferably di Gaeta)
>
> 2tsp capers, in brine
>
> 1 chilli pepper
>
> 1 small onion
>
> 3 garlic cloves
>
> 400g spaghetti
>
> 4tsp salt

1. Peel and finely chop the onion
2. Peel and slit the garlic cloves lengthways, leaving them whole
3. Crush the chilli pepper
4. In a heavy-bottomed saucepan, soften the onion, the chilli pepper and the garlic in the olive oil for a few minutes without browning
5. Add the peeled tomatoes, olives and capers, along with 400ml water and allow to cook for about 2 hours, stirring occasionally
6. When the sauce is cooked, remove and discard the garlic cloves
7. Check for salt, adding some if necessary, and stir well
8. In a large saucepan, add 4tsp salt to 3lt water and bring to the boil
9. Throw the spaghetti into the boiling water and cook for 12–15 minutes, stirring frequently
10. Drain the spaghetti well and coat with the 'whore's' sauce
11. Serve immediately

Di Gaeta olives – Gaeta is a place in Lazio where this type of olive comes from. They are neither green nor black, but a sort of purplish colour. They are usually sold in jars in brine, and should be found in most Italian delis. However, if you cannot find di Gaeta olives, any small olives in brine would also be suitable.

The theory behind the name of this dish is that in the past, when fast food did not exist, the 'ladies of the night' would prepare this quick pasta sauce of which the ingredients are all ready-made preserved food, so as not to waste too much time between clients!

ZITI WITH TOMATO SAUCE AND GREEN BEANS

Ziti al Sugo con Piattoni

400g large flat green beans (alternatively, French green beans)

1 small onion

50ml Italian extra-virgin olive oil

1 400g can peeled tomatoes

1 garlic clove

5tsp salt

400g long, large pasta tubes (ziti) or spaghetti

---

1. Top and tail the beans, wash well and cut into 2cm pieces
2. Peel and finely chop the onion
3. Peel and slit the garlic clove lengthways, leaving it whole
4. In a heavy-bottomed saucepan, soften the chopped onion and the garlic clove in the oil for a few minutes without browning
5. Add the peeled tomatoes, 400ml water and 1tsp salt
6. Cook through on low heat for about 2 hours, stirring occasionally
7. Remove and discard the garlic clove
8. In a large saucepan, add 4tsp salt to 3lt water and bring to the boil
9. Add the beans and cook for about 10 minutes
10. Using a slotted spoon, take out the green beans (do not discard the water) and put them into the tomato sauce; continue cooking for about another hour
11. With your hands, break up the *ziti* into uneven pieces
12. Bring the water left over from the beans to the boil and add the pieces of broken *ziti*, and cook for 12–15 minutes, stirring frequently

13. Drain well and return to the large saucepan
14. Add the tomato and bean sauce and stir well
15. Serve immediately

RICE

ARTICHOKE RISOTTO

Risotto ai Carciofi

---

8 globe artichokes

50ml Italian extra-virgin olive oil

400g Italian carnaroli or arborio rice

300ml dry white wine

2tsp salt

700ml vegetable stock

Chopped parsley

1 lemon

---

1. Chop off the top and stalk of each artichoke and remove all the outer leaves, leaving only the innermost heart
2. Put 1lt water into a large bowl and squeeze in the lemon juice
3. Slice the artichoke hearts as thinly as possible (if there is any 'beard' in the centre, discard this too) and immediately plunge the slices into the lemon water, to prevent them from going black
4. In a large heavy-bottomed frying pan, heat the olive oil
5. Add the drained artichoke slices and salt and fry for a few minutes, stirring frequently
6. Reduce the heat, cover and allow the artichokes to sweat for about 10 minutes, stirring occasionally
7. Add the rice to the artichokes and fry for a few minutes, stirring frequently
8. Add the white wine and cook until absorbed, stirring well
9. Gradually add the stock, stirring continuously
10. Continue adding the stock until the rice has soaked it all up
11. If the rice is not quite cooked, add hot water a little at a time, stirring well, until nice and plump
12. Sprinkle the rice with a little chopped parsley and serve

ASPARAGUS RISOTTO

Risotto agli Asparagi

> 1kg fresh asparagus spears
> 75ml Italian extra-virgin olive oil
> 200ml dry white wine
> 800ml vegetable stock
> 400g Italian carnaroli or arborio rice
> 1tsp chopped parsley
> 1–2tsp salt

1. Wash the asparagus spears well, chop off the very hard, dry ends and discard
2. Cut off the tips of the spears and leave to soak in cold water
3. Chop the rest of the spears into small discs, about ½cm in thickness
4. In a very large heavy-bottomed frying pan, soften the asparagus discs in the olive oil with 1tsp salt for a few minutes without browning
5. Reduce the heat and cover, allowing the asparagus to sweat for about 15 minutes, stirring occasionally
6. Drain the tips, add these and continue to cook for about another 10 minutes
7. Add the rice and fry for a few minutes, stirring frequently
8. Add the white wine, stir well and cook through
9. Add a little broth to the rice and stir until the rice has soaked it all up
10. Continue adding broth, a little at a time, keeping the heat low, until the rice has soaked it all up
11. Check that the rice is cooked, adding more hot water, a little at a time, if necessary

12. Add salt if needed and stir well
13. Add chopped parsley and stir well
14. Leave to stand for about 5 minutes before serving

This is a very delicate risotto, so accompany it with a delicate white wine.

FENNEL RISOTTO

Risotto ai Finocchi

1kg fennel

1 small onion

400g Italian carnaroli or arborio rice

200ml dry white wine

50ml Italian extra-virgin olive oil

800ml vegetable stock

1–2tsp salt

---

1. Peel and very finely slice the onion
2. Remove and discard the outer parts of the fennel, retaining only the central bulbs
3. Wash the fennel bulbs and slice as finely as possible
4. In a large heavy-bottomed frying pan, soften the sliced onion and fennel in the olive oil for a few minutes without browning
5. Add 1tsp salt, cover with a tight-fitting lid and lower the heat
6. Allow the fennel to sweat for about 30–40 minutes, stirring occasionally
7. When the fennel has softened, add the rice
8. Raise the heat and fry for a few minutes, stirring frequently
9. Add the white wine and cook through, stirring frequently
10. Gradually add the hot stock, a little at a time, stirring at each addition, until the rice has soaked up all the stock
11. Check to see if the rice is cooked; if necessary, add more hot water, a little at a time
12. Taste for salt, adding a little if necessary, and give a final stir
13. Serve immediately

RED RADICCHIO RISOTTO

Risotto al Radicchio

500g red radicchio

400g Italian carnaroli or arborio rice

75ml Italian extra-virgin olive oil

300ml red wine

700ml vegetable stock

1tsp salt

Black pepper to taste

---

1. Wash the radicchio well and roughly shred
2. In a large heavy-bottomed frying pan, soften the shredded radicchio in the olive oil and salt for a few minutes
3. When the radicchio has begun to wilt, add the rice
4. Fry for a few minutes, stirring frequently, then add the red wine
5. Cook through, stirring frequently
6. Gradually add the hot stock, stirring very frequently
7. Continue adding the stock until the rice has soaked it all up
8. If the rice is not quite cooked, add more hot water, a little at a time, stirring all the time
9. Check for salt, adding a little if necessary and mixing in well
10. Serve with a dash of freshly milled black pepper

RICE BALLS

Arancini di Riso

300g Italian carnaroli or arborio rice

200g tinned garden peas

1 small onion

1 garlic clove

1 400g can chopped tomatoes

1tsp chopped parsley

50g plain flour

100g fine breadcrumbs

50ml Italian extra-virgin olive oil

3tsp salt

1lt corn oil

1. Peel and finely chop the onion

2. Peel and slit the garlic clove lengthways, leaving it whole

3. In a large heavy-bottomed saucepan, soften the onion and the garlic in the olive oil for a few minutes without browning

4. Add the can of chopped tomatoes, 400ml water and 2tsp salt

5. Cook the tomatoes through on a low heat for about 2 hours, stirring occasionally

6. When cooked, remove and discard the garlic clove

7. In a separate saucepan, add 1tsp salt to 1lt water and bring to the boil

8. Add the rice and boil for about 8–10 minutes (the rice should be a little underdone)

9. Drain the rice well and add to the tomato sauce, mixing evenly

10. Remove from the heat

11. Drain the peas and add these to the rice along with the chopped parsley and stir gently

12. Leave aside to cool completely

13. When the rice is completely cold, add the flour

14. Mix very well with your hands, squashing the rice (it doesn't matter if a few peas get squashed as well)

15. Using your hands, form balls of about 6cm in diameter; they should be very compact and a little sticky

16. Roll the balls in the breadcrumbs making sure they are coated well

17. In a deep frying pan heat the corn oil until it is very hot

18. Deep-fry the rice balls for about 5–7 minutes, until they are golden

19. Serve on absorbent kitchen paper

These rice balls are very popular to take on picnics, and they are commonly found in takeaway outlets in the centre and south of Italy.

RICE SALAD

Insalata di Riso

300g parboiled Italian ribe rice

300g canned sweetcorn

300g canned garden peas

150g stoned black olives

150g white mini pickled cocktail onions

150g cocktail button mushrooms, in oil

200g split artichoke hearts, in oil

200g pickled red peppers, in brine

100ml white wine vinegar

100ml Italian extra-virgin olive oil

1tsp salt

---

1. Add the rice and salt to 1½lt water and boil for about 10–12 minutes until the rice is slightly undercooked
2. Drain thoroughly
3. In a large bowl, combine the vinegar and hot rice, mixing well
4. Drain and finely dice the red peppers
5. Drain the sweetcorn and the peas and add to the rice, together with the whole olives, onions, mushrooms, peppers and artichoke hearts, then mix well
6. Add the olive oil
7. Taste for salt and, if necessary, stir in a little
8. Leave aside for a few hours at room temperature and serve

This is a summertime favourite – it is light and refreshing and a must at family picnics.

RISOTTO WITH WILD MUSHROOMS

Risotto ai Funghi Porcini

25g wild dried porcini (boletus edilus) mushrooms

1 small onion

50ml olive oil (not extra-virgin)

1 garlic clove

600ml vegetable stock

250ml dry white wine

1tsp chopped parsley

400g Italian carnaroli or arborio rice

1–2tsp Salt

Black pepper to taste

---

1. Soak the mushrooms in 150ml very hot water and leave aside
2. Peel and very finely slice the onion and peel and slit the garlic clove lengthways, leaving it whole
3. Drain the mushrooms but retain the dark water that they soaked in
4. Roughly chop the mushrooms
5. In a very large heavy-bottomed frying pan, soften the onion and garlic in the olive oil with 1tsp salt for a few minutes and then add the chopped mushrooms
6. Cover with a lid and sweat for about 15 minutes or until the onions are transparent
7. Discard the garlic clove
8. Add the rice to the frying pan and, on a high heat, fry for a few seconds, stirring frequently
9. Add the wine and cook through for a few minutes

10. Strain the dark water from the soaked mushrooms and add to the rice and cook through

11. Add a little stock and cook through

12. Continue adding the stock to the rice a little at a time, stirring frequently

13. When the rice has soaked up all the stock, check if it is cooked; if not, gradually add hot water, stirring all the time

14. When the rice is cooked, add the chopped parsley, salt to taste and stir well

15. Sprinkle with a little black pepper before serving

YELLOW SAFFRON RICE

Riso Giallo allo Zafferano

400g Italian carnaroli or arborio rice

50ml Italian extra-virgin olive oil

1 large onion

400ml dry white wine

600ml vegetable stock

1tsp powdered saffron

1–2tsp salt

Black pepper to taste

---

1. Peel the onion and slice thickly
2. In a teacup, dissolve the powdered saffron in a little water
3. In a large heavy-bottomed frying pan, soften the onion slices in the oil with 1tsp salt for a few minutes without browning
4. Cover the frying pan with a lid and lower the heat
5. Sweat the onions in the oil for about 15 minutes, stirring occasionally
6. Remove the onions with a slotted spoon and discard
7. Raise the heat and throw the rice into the hot oil
8. Fry for a few minutes, stirring frequently, then add the white wine
9. Cook through, stirring frequently
10. Gradually add the hot stock, stirring continuously
11. When the rice has soaked up all the stock, add the saffron and stir well
12. If the rice is not quite cooked, add a little hot water a little at a time, until it is all soaked up
13. Taste for salt, adding if necessary, and give the rice a final stir
14. Serve with freshly milled black pepper

POLENTA, GNOCCHI AND BARLEY

BARLEY RISOTTO

Orzotto

500g pearl barley

2 carrots

1 small onion

3 sticks celery

50ml corn oil

1lt strong vegetable stock

1tsp chopped parsley

Black pepper to taste

---

1. Peel the carrots and the onion and chop very finely
2. Wash the celery sticks and slice as finely as possible
3. Heat the oil in a very large heavy-bottomed saucepan and add the chopped vegetables
4. Fry for a few minutes, stirring frequently, then add 100ml water
5. Cover with a tight-fitting lid and allow to cook gently for about 30 minutes, stirring occasionally
6. Add the barley to the vegetables and fry for a few minutes, stirring frequently
7. Add the stock and stir well
8. Cover with a lid and allow to cook for about 1 hour, stirring occasionally, until the barley has soaked up all the broth
9. Before serving, sprinkle with 1tsp chopped parsley and, if liked, a dash of black pepper

This is a very old, northern Italian mountain dish – from the days when they didn't have much else!

'CHASE THE CATS!'

Cassagatti

> *500g polenta (cornmeal)*
>
> *1 400g can Italian borlotti beans*
>
> *50ml corn oil*
>
> *1 400g can peeled tomatoes*
>
> *1 small onion*
>
> *4tsp salt*

1. Peel and finely chop the onion
2. In a heavy-bottomed saucepan, soften the onion in the oil for a few minutes without browning
3. Add the tomatoes, 1tsp salt and 400ml water
4. Allow to cook for about 1 hour, stirring occasionally
5. In the meantime, in a large saucepan, add 3tsp salt to 2lt water and heat gently
6. When the water is lukewarm, pour in the polenta flour
7. Stir vigorously and continue stirring over a gentle heat until it begins to thicken
8. Cook for about 30 minutes, stirring frequently
9. Add the can of borlotti beans together with the liquid in the can and the tomato sauce
10. Stir well and continue cooking for about 40 minutes
11. Allow to stand for a few minutes before serving

The story behind the name of this dish says that, in the old days, the polenta used to be put to cook on the wood stove – this was also the favourite place for the cats to sit where it was nice and warm. The polenta, however, would reach very high temperatures and bubble violently, and sometimes splashes of boiling hot polenta resembling volcanic lava would touch the cats, making them scurry away screeching!

GRANDMA'S MINI GREEN GNOCCHI

Chicche della Nonna

500g fresh spinach (or 250g frozen)

1kg potatoes

Approx. 350g plain flour

1 small onion

1 garlic clove

1 400g can chopped tomatoes

50ml Italian extra-virgin olive oil

6tsp salt

Extra flour for dusting

---

1. Peel and cut the potatoes into even pieces

2. Boil in unsalted water for about 20 minutes

3. If using fresh spinach, wash very well

4. Put the spinach, fresh or frozen, into a dry saucepan over a moderate heat for about 10–15 minutes, stirring occasionally

5. Drain the potatoes and immediately mash, then transfer to a large bowl

6. Drain the spinach (if necessary) and chop up as finely as possible, preferably in a food processor

7. Add the spinach to the potatoes, together with the flour and 1tsp salt

8. Mix well, adding more flour if necessary, until the dough is compact and smooth – not sticky

9. Prepare two large trays with clean tea towels and dust with flour

10. With your hands well floured, pick small pieces of potato mixture from the bowl and form little balls, about the size of a hazelnut

11. Place each little ball onto the floured tray

12. Continue making little *chicche* until all the dough is used up

13. Cover the trays with clean, dry tea towels and set aside in a cool, dry place (not the fridge)

14. Peel and finely chop the onion

15. Peel and slit the garlic clove lengthways, leaving it whole

16. In a heavy-bottomed saucepan, soften the onion and garlic in the olive oil for a few minutes without browning

17. Add the chopped tomatoes and 400ml water and 1tsp salt

18. Cook the sauce for about 2 hours over a moderate heat, stirring frequently

19. When the sauce is cooked, remove and discard the garlic clove

20. In a large saucepan, add 4tsp salt to 3lt water and bring to the boil

21. Throw in all the *chicche* and stir well

22. As the *chicche* surface, scoop them out with a slotted spoon and place in a large serving bowl

23. Spoon a little of the tomato sauce over the top and stir

24. When the *chicche* are all cooked, spoon over all the tomato sauce and give a final stir

25. Serve immediately

POLENTA WITH CABBAGE AND BEANS

Polenta Incatenata

300g cabbage

1 400g can Italian borlotti beans

1 small onion

25ml Italian extra-virgin olive oil

150g polenta flour (cornmeal)

3tsp salt

Black pepper to taste

---

1. Wash and finely shred the cabbage
2. Peel and chop the onion
3. In a large saucepan, sweat the onion in the olive oil with 1tsp salt over a gentle heat for about 10 minutes, until soft but not browned
4. Add the shredded cabbage and 1 cup water and cook slowly, stirring occasionally for about 30 minutes
5. Drain the borlotti beans and add these to the saucepan and cook through for a further 5 minutes
6. In a larger saucepan, add 2tsp salt to 1½lt water and bring to the boil
7. Add the bean and cabbage mixture to the water and cook for about 15 minutes
8. Using a long wooden spoon, start stirring the mixture and at the same time pour in the polenta flour, taking care to keep stirring so as to avoid the formation of lumps
9. Keep stirring until the water has absorbed the flour well without lumps
10. Lower the heat and allow to cook on a gentle heat for about 40 minutes, stirring very frequently
11. Serve topped with a drizzle of Italian extra-virgin olive oil and freshly milled black pepper

POLENTA WITH WILD MUSHROOM SAUCE

Polenta con i Funghi Porcini

30g dried porcini (boletus edilus) mushrooms

50g olive oil (not extra-virgin)

1 small onion

2 garlic cloves

2 400g tins peeled tomatoes

1tsp chopped parsley

500g polenta (cornmeal)

4tsp salt

---

1. Soak the mushrooms in 100ml very hot water and leave aside
2. Peel and finely chop the onion
3. Peel and slit the garlic cloves lengthways, leaving them whole
4. In a large heavy-bottomed saucepan, soften the onion and garlic in the olive oil for a few minutes without browning
5. Drain the mushrooms but retain the water in which they have been soaking
6. Add the mushrooms to the saucepan and fry for a few minutes, stirring frequently
7. Pour the dark water from the soaked mushrooms through a fine strainer and add to the saucepan
8. Add the tomatoes together with 800ml water, the chopped parsley and 2tsp salt
9. Simmer, uncovered, for 2–3 hours, stirring occasionally, until the sauce is thick and rich
10. Remove and discard the garlic

11. In a large saucepan, add 2tsp salt to 2lt water and place on a medium heat

12. When the water is hand-hot, pour in the polenta flour, mixing well and ensuring no lumps form; if necessary, use a whisk

13. Continue heating, stirring continuously, until the mixture comes to a boil, then lower to a simmer

14. Cook the polenta for about 40 minutes, stirring very frequently

15. When the polenta is cooked, place on a large serving dish, leaving a dip in the centre for the mushroom sauce

16. Put the mushroom sauce in the centre and serve piping hot

TRUFFLE GNOCCHI

Gnocchi al Tartufo

1kg potatoes

350g plain flour

1 black (or white) truffle

Approx. 50ml Italian extra-virgin olive oil

5tsp salt

Extra flour for dusting

---

1. Peel and cut the potatoes into even-sized pieces, then boil in unsalted water for about 20 minutes

2. Drain the potatoes and mash

3. In a large bowl, place the flour and 1tsp salt and add the mashed potatoes, mixing well

4. Knead until you get a smooth dough

5. Prepare a large tray with a clean tea towel and dust with flour

6. With you hands dusted with flour, pick out a small amount of dough and form a little ball about 1½cm in diameter and place on the floured tea towel

7. Continue forming little balls until all the dough is used up

8. In a large saucepan, add 4tsp salt to 3lt water and bring to the boil

9. Throw all the gnocchi balls in at once and stir gently for a few seconds

10. As they surface, remove with a slotted spoon and place in large serving bowl

11. Dress each layer with a dribble of olive oil and some grated truffle

12. Continue with all the gnocchi finishing off with a top layer of truffle

13. Serve immediately

PIZZAS, PIES AND SNACKS

AUBERGINE ROLY-POLY

Arrotolato di Melanzane

250g strong flour

250g plain flour

1 packet active baking yeast

1tsp sugar

3 medium-sized aubergines

1 400g can peeled tomatoes

2 garlic cloves

100ml Italian extra-virgin olive oil

3tsp salt

Flour for dusting

Oil for greasing

---

1. Mix the flours with the sugar, yeast and 2tsp salt

2. Add warm water and 50ml olive oil, a little at a time, and gradually work the mixture into a firm, smooth ball

3. Cover the ball with a plastic bag, ensuring that it does not touch the dough, and leave aside for at least three hours until the dough has doubled in size

4. Wash and dice the aubergines

5. Peel and slit the garlic cloves lengthways, leaving them whole, and place in a large frying pan with the remaining oil

6. Fry the garlic for a few minutes and then remove and discard

7. Add the chopped aubergines to the oil, along with the peeled tomatoes and 1tsp salt

8. Cook slowly for about 2 hours on a low heat until the aubergines are soft and there is no water left, then allow to cool

9. Using well-floured hands, punch the dough back to its original size and knead for a few minutes until it is silky smooth; then roll out to form a large rectangle

10. Place the aubergine mixture in the centre of the rolled out dough and spread out to about 2 cm from the edges

11. Starting from the longest side of the rectangle, roll up like a Swiss roll, sealing the edges

12. Place the roly-poly onto a well-oiled, flat baking tray

13. Heat the oven to its highest temperature and cook the roly-poly for about 30 minutes

14. Allow to cool and then slice to serve

CHICKPEA ROUND

Farinata di Ceci

> *500g chickpea flour*
> *40ml Italian extra-virgin olive oil*
> *2tsp salt*

1. Put the flour into a large bowl and add 1½lt cold water, stirring all the time
2. Add the olive oil and 2tsp salt
3. Mix well until a smooth batter has formed
4. Leave aside for 1 hour, stirring occasionally to ensure no lumps form
5. Pour the batter into a large (40cm diameter) round cake tin
6. Bake in a hot oven for about 30 minutes until it begins to brown
7. Allow to cool completely before slicing

Serve as a snack, together with salads, olives etc.

CURLY ENDIVE PIZZA PIE

Calzone con Scarola

1kg curly endive lettuce

3 garlic cloves

100g olives, in brine – preferably olive di Gaeta

50g pine nuts

50g sultanas

3tsp capers, in brine

100ml Italian extra-virgin olive oil

250g plain flour

250g strong flour

1 sachet dried baker's yeast

1tsp sugar

3tsp salt

Flour for dusting

Oil for greasing

---

1. Cut the leaves off the thick stalk at the base of the endive and wash the leaves well

2. Place the washed endive leaves in a very large saucepan with 1tsp salt, and sweat over a moderate heat until they reduce by half in volume

3. Peel and slit the garlic cloves lengthways

4. If necessary, stone the olives – note: it is unimportant if the olives remain whole or not

5. Add 50ml olive oil to the saucepan together with the olives, the garlic, pine nuts, sultanas and capers

6. Allow to cook uncovered on a gentle heat for about 2–3 hours, stirring occasionally, until there is no water left

7. When completely cooked, leave aside to cool and remove and discard the garlic cloves

8. Meanwhile, make the pizza dough by combining the flours, sugar, yeast and 2tsp salt in a large bowl

9. Gradually add 50ml olive oil and warm water until you form a smooth round ball

10. Knead the dough until it is completely smooth

11. Cover the bowl with a plastic bag, ensuring that it does not touch the dough, and leave aside for about 3 hours or until the dough has doubled in size

12. Knead again for a few minutes, to knock it back to its original size

13. Roll the pizza dough out on a well-floured surface to a large round, about 50 cm in diameter

14. Brush some olive oil onto a 30cm pizza tray and place the dough on this, leaving the edges hanging over the edge of the tray

15. Place the cooled endive in the centre and fold over the dough to completely cover the endive

16. Prick the pizza pie all over with a fork

17. Heat the oven to its highest temperature, then put the pizza pie in and allow to cook for about 20–30 minutes or until the pie is a golden colour

18. Allow to cool a little before serving as this will enable you to cut it more easily

PIZZA MARINARA

> 500g strong flour
>
> 500g plain flour
>
> 4tsp salt
>
> 1tsp sugar
>
> 2 sachets dried baker's yeast
>
> 750g crushed tomatoes (passata grossa)
>
> 100ml Italian extra-virgin olive oil
>
> 2tsp dried oregano
>
> Flour for dusting
>
> Oil for greasing

1. Place the flours, salt, sugar and yeast all together in a very large bowl and mix thoroughly
2. Add about two cups lukewarm water and mix in
3. Form a ball with the dough, adding more water if necessary or adding more plain flour, until it is no longer sticky
4. Knead the dough for about five minutes until it is perfectly smooth
5. Cover the bowl with a plastic bag, ensuring that it does not touch the dough, and leave aside for about 3 hours until the dough has doubled in size
6. Knead again lightly and return to its bowl for another half an hour
7. After this time, take the dough out of the bowl and place on a large worktop or the kitchen table
8. Cut the dough into four equal parts
9. Using some plain flour to dust, roll out the dough into four 30cm-diameter rounds and place on well-oiled pizza baking trays
10. Spread the crushed tomato all over the dough
11. Drizzle the oil over all the tomato and sprinkle with oregano

12. Set the oven to its highest temperature

13. Cook the pizzas for about 15 minutes or until the crust has begun to brown

14. Serve immediately

Variations on the toppings can, of course, be added to customise your pizza – olives, sliced peppers, thinly sliced onion rings, sliced courgettes, artichoke hearts, garlic cloves, etc., although then it will no longer be a traditional pizza marinara.

If you want, do as the Italians do and drizzle some chilli oil over the pizza before eating for a bit of extra heat!

POTATO AND COURGETTE PIE

Torta di Patate e Zucchine

1kg potatoes

2 large onions

500g courgette

100ml corn oil

100ml olive oil (not extra-virgin)

500g plain flour

2tsp salt

Extra oil for greasing

Flour for dusting

---

1. Peel the potatoes and cut into even-sized pieces
2. Peel the onions and slice as thinly as possible
3. Wash the courgettes and slice into very thin discs
4. In a large heavy-bottomed saucepan, fry the courgettes and the onions in the corn oil together with 1tsp salt for a few minutes
5. Lower the heat and cover with a lid
6. Allow the onions and courgettes to cook for about 1 hour, stirring occasionally, until there is very little water left and they become mushy
7. Boil the potatoes in unsalted water for about 20 minutes
8. When the potatoes are cooked, immediately mash them and put into a large bowl
9. Add the stewed courgette and onion mixture, along with 1tsp salt, and mix well
10. Put the flour into a large bowl and form a well in the centre
11. Pour the olive oil into the well and gradually incorporate into the flour

12. Add enough cold water to form a dough

13. Knead until the dough is compact and smooth

14. Lightly oil a large rectangular baking tray

15. Roll out the pastry as thinly as possible into a large rectangle

16. Line the baking tray with the pastry, ensuring there is enough pastry hanging over the edge to be able to completely cover the pie

17. Spoon the mixture into the pasty case and press down firmly with your fingers

18. Fold over the overlapping pastry to completely cover the filling

19. Prick the pie all over with a fork

20. Brush with a little olive oil

21. Bake in a hot oven for about 40–50 minutes until the pastry is golden

22. Allow to cool a little before serving as this will enable you to cut it more easily

This is extremely good eaten cold and is ideal for picnics.

POTATO PIE

Torta di Patate

2kg potatoes

500g leeks

150ml corn oil

500g plain flour

3tsp salt

Oil for greasing

Flour for dusting

---

1. Wash the leeks thoroughly, and discard any discoloured leaves
2. Cut the leeks into 3cm long pieces
3. In a heavy-bottomed saucepan, fry the sliced leeks in the oil with 1tsp salt
4. Cook very gently with a lid for about 1 hour or until the leeks become soft, stirring occasionally
5. Peel and cut the potatoes into even-sized pieces
6. Boil the potatoes in unsalted water for about 30 minutes, then drain them very well and mash immediately
7. Add the cooked leeks and 2tsp salt and mix until the mash becomes smooth
8. In a large bowl, place the flour and slowly add cold water until you obtain a smooth dough
9. Roll out the dough on a well-floured work surface as thinly as possible
10. Grease a large flat baking tray with some oil
11. Line the tray with the dough, leaving the excess to hang over the sides
12. Spread the potato mixture evenly over the pastry

13. Fold over the overlapping dough to partly cover the potato and flatten down with your hands to secure

14. Brush over with a little oil

15. Prick the pie all over with a fork

16. Place in a hot oven for about 1 hour until the pastry is golden

17. Before serving, allow to cool a little as this will enable you to cut it more easily

POTATO PIZZA

Pizza di Patate

> *1kg potato*
>
> *100g stoned black olives*
>
> *50g capers, in brine*
>
> *1 400g can peeled whole tomatoes*
>
> *1 small onion*
>
> *75ml extra-virgin olive oil*
>
> *2tsp salt*
>
> *Extra oil for greasing*

1. Peel and cut the potatoes into even-sized pieces
2. Boil the potatoes in unsalted water for about 20–30 minutes
3. Immediately mash and place in a large bowl
4. Add 25ml of the olive oil and 1tsp salt and combine evenly
5. Peel and finely slice the onion
6. In a heavy-bottomed saucepan, soften the onion in the rest of the olive oil for a few minutes without browning
7. Add the can of peeled tomatoes and 1tsp salt
8. Cook through on a low heat for about 30 minutes, stirring occasionally
9. Lightly oil a large deep baking tray (5–6cm deep is ideal)
10. Put half the mashed potato into the tray and spread evenly
11. Cover with the tomato sauce and scatter the chopped olives and the drained capers over the tomato
12. Top with the remaining mashed potato
13. Drizzle some olive oil over the top

14. Bake in a hot oven for about 30 minutes until the top is golden
15. Serve hot

This is a typical dish of the Puglia area of Italy – very simple, but very good!

RED RADICCHIO PIZZA PIE

Calzone al Radicchio

1kg red radicchio

250g plain flour

250g strong flour

1 sachet dried active baking yeast

1tsp sugar

100ml Italian extra-virgin olive oil

50g stoned black olives

50g capers in brine

3tsp salt

Extra flour for dusting

Oil for greasing

---

1. Wash the radicchio well and shred

2. In a large heavy-bottomed frying pan, fry the radicchio in the olive oil with 1tsp salt for a few minutes

3. Allow to cook on a gentle heat for about 30–40 minutes until the radicchio is soft

4. Put the flours, yeast, sugar and 2tsp salt in a bowl and mix well

5. Gradually add warm water to form a dough

6. Knead the dough for about 10 minutes until it is smooth and no longer sticky

7. Cover the bowl with a plastic bag, ensuring that it does not touch the dough, and leave aside in a warm place for at least 3 hours or until it has doubled in size

8. Knock the dough back by dusting generously with flour and kneading it for a second time until it returns to its original size

9. Roll out two discs, about 40cm in diameter
10. Lightly oil a 30cm cake tin and line with one of the discs
11. Place the cooked radicchio into the centre and scatter the olives and the capers over the top
12. Put the other disc of dough over the radicchio and seal around the edges with your fingers
13. Prick all over with a fork and lightly brush with a little oil
14. Place in a hot oven for about 40–50 minutes until it is golden
15. Allow to cool a little before serving as this will enable you to cut it more easily

Radicchio can be quite bitter in taste, but it's certainly one worth acquiring!

ROSEMARY FOCACCIA

Focaccia al Rosmarino

400g plain flour

400g strong flour

1 sachet dried active baking yeast

1tsp sugar

100ml Italian extra-virgin olive oil

4 sprigs fresh rosemary

2tsp coarse salt

2tsp salt

Oil for greasing

Extra flour for dusting

---

1. In a large bowl place the flours, dried yeast, sugar and salt and mix very well

2. Gradually incorporate the olive oil together with enough warm water to form a firm dough

3. Using extra flour, knead the dough for about 5–10 minutes until it is smooth and no longer sticky

4. Cut the dough into two pieces

5. Brush two large rectangular baking trays with a little oil

6. Roll out each piece of dough into a rectangle, about 1cm thick, and place on their own tray, spreading out with your fingers

7. Prick all over with a fork

8. Detach the rosemary needles from the branch and generously sprinkle over the trays of dough

9. Sprinkle the coarse salt over each tray

10. Cover the trays with a damp tea towel, ensuring that it does not touch the dough, and leave aside in a warm place for about 3 hours; after this time, the dough should have risen a little

11. Heat the oven to its highest temperature, and bake for 10–15 minutes until they begin to turn a golden brown

12. Serve warm if possible, but this focaccia is also excellent cold

A popular variation on this is to use stoned green olives instead of the rosemary. You might also want to try it topped with very thinly sliced onion.

SAVOURY TOAST

Bruschette

1 loaf pugliese bread, (or Greek-style bread)
50ml Italian extra-virgin olive oil
4 garlic cloves
2tsp oregano
500g fresh ripe tomatoes
1tsp salt

1. Chop the tomatoes and combine in a bowl with the oregano, oil and salt
2. Slice the bread and toast
3. Peel the garlic and rub onto each slice of toast, while still hot
4. Spoon the tomato mixture with its juice onto each slice of toast
5. Serve while still warm

It is important not to use a type of bread that is too soft when making bruschette.

SPINACH PIE

Torta d'Erbe

500g flat leaf spinach

100ml Italian extra-virgin olive oil

600g plain flour

3tsp salt

Extra oil for greasing

Flour for dusting

---

1. Wash the spinach leaves thoroughly and allow to drain
2. Mix the flour and 1tsp salt together with enough cold water to make a firm dough
3. Roll out the pasty as thinly as possible, then transfer onto a large, well-oiled flat baking tray, leaving about 6–7cm of pastry hanging over the outer rim of the tray
4. When the spinach is dry, chop the leaves and place into a large mixing bowl, sprinkle with 2tsp salt and the oil, then combine well
5. Place the spinach mixture into the centre of the pastry case and wrap, leaving the centre uncovered
6. Press the dough down on the spinach mixture to secure and smooth over the pastry with a little oil
7. With a fork, prick the pastry all over
8. Cook in moderate oven for about 1 hour or until the base is well cooked
9. Allow to cool completely before serving
10. When serving, slice into squares

Make sure you give everyone a serviette as the oil drips when you bite!

VEGETABLES

AUBERGINE STEW

La Caponata

> 2kg large, round, purple aubergines
>
> 300g celery
>
> 100g stoned green olives
>
> 2tsp capers, in brine
>
> 50g pine nuts
>
> 1tsp sugar
>
> 100ml white wine vinegar
>
> 1 handful fresh basil leaves
>
> 75ml Italian extra-virgin olive oil
>
> 3tsp coarse salt
>
> Salt to taste

1. Wash the aubergines well and cut into 2cm chunks
2. Put the aubergine chunks into a large bowl with coarse salt and toss
3. Leave the bowl aside for about 3 hours, tossing occasionally
4. Wash the celery well and cut into pieces about 2cm long
5. Boil the celery pieces in unsalted water for about 10 minutes, until they have softened a little
6. Drain the celery and set aside
7. Roughly chop the olives and drain the capers
8. Wash and roughly chop the basil leaves
9. Drain the aubergine chunks from the dark water
10. Wash them well in a large bowl, then squeeze each handful so that you get most of the liquid out

11. Place all the aubergine chunks into a large colander and allow to drain

12. In a very large heavy-bottomed frying pan, heat the olive oil to sizzling

13. Set the aubergine chunks evenly around the pan, taking care not to splash the oil

14. Allow to cook for a few minutes, stirring continuously, then lower the heat

15. Stir in the celery pieces, chopped olives, capers, pine nuts and chopped basil

16. Allow to cook through gently on a low heat for about 1 hour, stirring occasionally

17. Taste for salt, adding if necessary

18. Remove from the heat and add the sugar and the vinegar and stir well

19. Allow to cool to room temperature before serving

BAKED AUBERGINES

Melanzane al Forno

1kg firm long aubergines

10 garlic cloves

100ml Italian extra-virgin olive oil

2 handfuls fresh basil leaves

1 400g can chopped tomatoes

1tsp dried oregano

1–2tsp salt

---

1. Wash the aubergines well and split in half lengthways
2. Place in a large rectangular oven dish, cut side up
3. Peel and cut the garlic cloves into small slices
4. Slit the flesh of each aubergine 3 or 4 times and insert a slice of garlic and a leaf of basil into each slit
5. Sprinkle with salt
6. Cover the aubergines with the tomatoes and olive oil and sprinkle with oregano
7. Place in a moderate oven and cook for about 1 hour, until the aubergines are soft
8. Serve very hot with fresh crusty bread

BAKED FENNEL

Finocchi al Forno

> *1kg fennel*
> *50g fine breadcrumbs*
> *2 sprigs fresh rosemary*
> *50ml Italian extra-virgin olive oil*
> *1tsp salt*

1. Trim the fennel well, discarding the outer parts of the bulb and the stalks
2. Wash the fennel bulbs and quarter
3. Boil the fennel in unsalted water for about 10 minutes
4. Drain and allow to cool
5. Detach the rosemary needles from the branch and chop as finely as possible
6. In a bowl, mix the chopped rosemary with the breadcrumbs and salt
7. In a shallow oven dish, lay out the fennel bulbs side by side, flat side up
8. Sprinkle with the breadcrumb mixture and drizzle with the olive oil
9. Bake in hot oven for about 20 minutes
10. Serve immediately

BEAN STEW

Fagioli in Umido

300g dried borlotti beans

1 small onion

2 carrots

1 stick celery

1 garlic clove

25ml Italian extra-virgin olive oil

1 400g can peeled tomatoes

1tsp chopped parsley

1tsp dried marjoram

2–3tsp Salt

black pepper to taste

---

1. Place the dried beans in a bowl of cold water and leave overnight, then drain and rinse thoroughly

2. Peel and finely slice the onion and the carrots

3. Wash and finely slice the celery

4. Peel and slit the garlic clove lengthways, leaving it whole

5. Soften the onion, carrots, celery and garlic in the oil for a few minutes, without browning

6. Add the beans and fry for a few minutes, stirring frequently

7. Remove the garlic clove and discard

8. Add the tomatoes and 400ml water together with the parsley and marjoram

9. Bring to the boil and then lower the heat and allow to simmer very gently for about 3 hours, stirring occasionally

10. Check if the beans are cooked and if so, add salt according to taste, and stir well

11. Sprinkle with black pepper and serve immediately, preferably with toasted bread

CHARGRILLED PEPPERS

Peperoni alla Griglia

1kg large plump red peppers

3 garlic cloves

100ml Italian extra-virgin olive oil

1tsp salt

---

1. Heat the oven to its highest temperature
2. Arrange the well-washed peppers on a baking tray and place them in the oven for about 40 minutes, turning them occasionally, until the skins begin to char
3. Carefully remove from the oven taking care not to burst them open
4. Allow to cool completely
5. Peel off all the skins and discard together with all the seeds and pith
6. Cut the peppers into thin strips and place in a large, flat dish
7. Peel and slit the garlic cloves lengthways, leaving them whole and add to the peppers
8. Add the oil and salt and mix well
9. Cover the dish and leave in a cool place (not the fridge) for about 3–4 hours
10. Before serving, discard the garlic cloves
11. Serve with fresh crusty bread for mopping up the very tasty oil

As the name suggests, these peppers are ideally blackened on a barbecue, but the above method is much simpler and the results are just as good.

CHIPS WITH PEPPERS

Patate con Peperoni

> 6 medium-sized potatoes
>
> 2 large red peppers
>
> 75ml Italian extra-virgin olive oil
>
> 1–2tsp salt

1. Peel and slice the potatoes into large chips
2. Core the peppers and slice into long strips
3. Heat the oil in a very large heavy-bottomed frying pan, then add the peppers and fry in the oil for about 15 minutes, stirring occasionally, until they begin to soften
4. Add the chips and continue frying at high heat for about 10 minutes
5. Lower the heat and allow to fry gently for about 1 hour, stirring occasionally
6. Salt according to taste and serve immediately

This simple dish may sound very plain, but if the peppers are of good quality, the taste is wonderful and when accompanied by some fresh bread it is a very satisfying meal.

In the south of Italy, this is a weekday supper dish. Large quantities are made to feed the hungry children of the family.

COURGETTE CHIPS

Zucchine Fritte

> *1kg courgettes*
>
> *1lt corn oil*
>
> *100g plain flour*
>
> *2tsp coarse salt*
>
> *Salt to taste*

1. Wash the courgettes and cut them into chips about 5cm in length
2. In a very large bowl, toss the courgette chips and coarse salt
3. Leave the bowl of courgettes aside for at least 3 hours or longer
4. Drain and rinse the courgettes in fresh water
5. Squeeze them and lay them out on a clean, dry tea towel to dry
6. Leave them to dry for about an hour
7. Coat the courgette chips with flour
8. Heat the corn oil in a large, deep frying pan
9. Deep-fry the courgettes for about 7–8 minutes until crisp
10. Drain on absorbent kitchen paper
11. Add a sprinkling of salt if needed
12. Serve immediately

'FLY THE FLAG' PLATTER

Teglia Tricolore

500g courgettes

2 large onions

2 large red peppers

50ml Italian extra-virgin olive oil

½ tsp dried thyme

1tsp salt

---

1. Wash the courgettes and slice lengthways
2. Peel the onions and slice into thin rings
3. Wash the peppers and carefully remove all the pith and pips from the inside, and cut into strips about 1cm thick
4. In a rectangular oven dish, lay out the vegetables starting from the left in this order: the slices of courgettes first, the onion rings in the middle, finishing with the strips of pepper to the right
6. Sprinkle over the dried thyme and salt
7. Pour over the olive oil
8. Cover with aluminium foil and bake in the oven at a moderate heat for about 1 hour
9. Remove the foil and return to the oven for another 30 minutes until the vegetables begin to brown
10. Serve either hot or cold

For patriots only!

FOIL-BAKED PUMPKIN

Zucca al Cartoccio

---

1 1kg pumpkin

50ml corn oil

1–2tsp salt

---

1. Slice the pumpkin into rounds, about 2cm thick
2. Scoop out all the seeds and pith from each slice
3. Slice off the hard skin
4. Place each ring of pumpkin in a piece of aluminium foil, together with a dribble of oil and a sprinkling of salt
5. Wrap up the piece of pumpkin to form a little parcel
6. Put all the parcels into a baking dish and bake in a hot oven for about 40–50 minutes
7. Serve in their foil

To give this dish an even more authentic flavour, cook the parcels in the fireplace.

FRIED COURGETTES WITH VINEGAR AND MINT

Zucchine a Scapec

> 1kg courgettes
>
> 2 garlic cloves
>
> 30ml Italian extra-virgin olive oil
>
> 20ml white wine vinegar
>
> 6 fresh mint leaves
>
> 2tsp coarse salt
>
> Salt to taste

1. Wash the courgettes and slice into thin discs
2. In a very large bowl, place the courgette discs and sprinkle with the coarse salt
3. Toss the courgettes well in the bowl and leave aside for at least 3 hours or longer
4. Discard any liquid that may have collected and rinse the courgettes with fresh water
5. Lay them out onto clean, dry tea towels to dry for about 1 hour
6. Peel and slit the garlic cloves lengthways, leaving them whole
7. In a large heavy-bottomed frying pan, fry the garlic cloves in the olive oil for a few minutes
8. Add the courgettes
9. Fry over a moderate heat for about 30 minutes, stirring frequently until they begin to brown
10. Remove and discard the garlic cloves
11. Chop the mint leaves
12. When the courgettes are cooked, add the vinegar and the chopped mint and taste for salt, adding a little if necessary
13. Serve either hot or cold

FRIED MUSHROOMS

Funghi Porcini Trifolati

> *500g fresh porcini (boletus edilus) mushrooms*
> *5 garlic cloves*
> *50ml olive oil (not extra-virgin)*
> *2tsp chopped parsley*
> *1tsp salt*

1. Clean the mushrooms with a tea towel to remove any dirt, but do not wash them
2. Slice them lengthways
3. Peel and slit the garlic cloves lengthways, leaving them whole
4. Put the oil into a large frying pan and fry the garlic for a few minutes, stirring frequently, without browning
5. Throw in the mushroom slices and fry on a high heat for a minute, stirring frequently, then lower the heat and add the chopped parsley and salt
6. Fry the mushrooms very gently for about 30 minutes, stirring occasionally, or until they begin to turn golden in colour and there is no liquid left
7. Hunt out the garlic cloves and discard
8. Serve with fresh bread – delicious!

Fresh porcini mushrooms can be hard to find in the UK. In Italy they are usually found growing wild in the woods of the Appenine mountains. You may be able to find them frozen in specialist shops, and this is a suitable alternative.

'GREENS' STEW

La Ribollita

300g day-old white bread

400g dried Italian white cannellini beans

300g Savoy cabbage

300g other greens, such as kale or spring greens

300g spinach

2 large potatoes

2 carrots

2 sticks celery

2 large onions

2tsp concentrated tomato paste

75ml Italian extra-virgin olive oil

2tsp salt

Black pepper to taste

---

1. Soak the cannellini beans overnight in cold water
2. Boil the beans in about 1½lt unsalted water for about 2 hours
3. With a slotted spoon, transfer the beans to another bowl and reserve the cooking water
4. Pass about 300g of the beans through a vegetable mill or a food processor and reduce to a paste
5. Return the bean mixture to the saucepan with the cooking water, stir and set aside
6. Peel and finely chop one of the onions and both carrots
7. Peel the potatoes and slice them thickly

8. Wash the celery sticks and finely slice

9. Wash and shred the various cabbages and spinach

10. Dissolve the concentrated tomato paste with a little hot water

11. In another very large heavy-bottomed saucepan, soften the chopped onion in the olive oil for a few minutes without browning and then add the tomato paste

12. Add the carrots, celery, potatoes and all the greens to the saucepan, along with the salt and fry for a few minutes, stirring frequently

13. Stir in the bean mixture with all the cooking liquid and lower the heat

14. Cover with a tight-fitting lid and let simmer gently for about 2 hours, stirring occasionally

15. Slice the bread and add to the vegetable mixture, together with the remaining beans

16. Allow to cook through for about 10 minutes, then remove from the heat and stir well, to combine all the ingredients

17. Peel and slice the other onion into very thin rings

18. Put the mixture into a large oven dish and cover with the onion rings, a drizzle of olive oil and some freshly milled black pepper

19. Bake in a very hot oven for about 30 minutes until the onion begins to brown

20. Allow to cool a little before serving

GRILLED AUBERGINES

Melanzane alla Griglia

1kg dark, plump aubergines

50ml Italian extra-virgin olive oil

1–2tsp Salt

---

1. Wash the aubergines and slice into discs about ½cm thick
2. Heat a griddle or barbecue until very hot
3. Place the slices of aubergine on the griddle and sprinkle with salt
4. Allow to brown a little and then turn the slices over and sprinkle again with salt
5. When they have browned on both sides, remove and place in a bowl
6. Allow to cool completely
7. When the aubergines are cold, add the olive oil and mix well

Serve as a light starter with some good bread

GRILLED COURGETTES

Zucchine alla Griglia

1kg medium-sized courgettes
100ml Italian extra-virgin olive oil
30ml white wine vinegar
1–2tsp salt

---

1. Wash the courgettes well and slice lengthways to a thickness of about 2mm

2. Place them on either a very hot heavy iron griddle or a barbecue

3. Sprinkle with salt

4. Allow them to brown a little but not burn

5. Turn each slice over and sprinkle with salt again

6. When they are all cooked, place in a large flat dish and, while still hot, add the vinegar

7. Allow to cool and then add the oil and mix well

8. Cover the dish and leave in a cool place (not the fridge) for about 3–4 hours

9. Serve with fresh crusty bread for mopping up the very tasty oil

RICE-STUFFED PEPPERS

Peperoni Ripieni al Riso

---

2 large, plump red peppers

2 large, plump yellow peppers

250g Italian carnaroli or arborio rice

1lt vegetable stock

1 400g can garden peas

1tsp concentrated tomato paste

25g fine breadcrumbs

50ml Italian extra-virgin olive oil

2tsp salt

---

1. Bring the stock to the boil and add the rice, together with the tomato paste
2. Cook the rice for no more than 5 minutes; it should still be rather hard
3. Drain the rice and place in a bowl with 25ml of the olive oil and 1tsp salt
4. Drain the peas and add these to the rice, mixing well
5. Wash the peppers and cut in half lengthways
6. Remove all the pith and pips inside and the tops
7. Place the peppers in an oven-proof dish side by side, cut side up
8. Spoon the rice into each pepper
9. Sprinkle each pepper with a little salt and some breadcrumbs and a good dribble of olive oil
10. Cover the dish with aluminium foil and put into a hot oven for about 40 minutes
11. Remove the aluminium foil and continue cooking for about a further 10 minutes until they are crusty on top
12. Allow to cool a little before serving

ROMAN ARTICHOKES

Carciofi alla Romana

---

10 globe artichokes, with part of the stalk still attached

2 lemons

100ml Italian extra-virgin olive oil

1tsp dried oregano

3tsp salt

---

1. Prepare a large bowl half-filled with cold water and the juice of one of the lemons
2. Strip the artichokes of all the outer leaves
3. Cut off most of the stalks, leaving about 2cm attached
4. Cut off the tops of the leaves, so that all that remains are the tender 'hearts' of the artichokes
5. Split each artichoke heart down the middle and remove any 'beard' that there may be
6. As you prepare each heart, plunge into the lemon water to prevent them from going black
7. In a large saucepan, add 2tsp salt to 2lt water and bring to the boil
8. Drain the artichokes and add to the saucepan, and boil for about 10 minutes
9. When they are tender, dry and lay out onto a clean, dry tea towel to dry out completely for about 1 hour
10. Combine the olive oil and the juice of the other lemon together with 1tsp salt and the oregano in a large bowl
11. Add the artichokes and mix well
12. Set aside in a cool place (not the fridge) for at least 3 hours
13. Serve cold at room temperature

SICILIAN-STYLE VEGETABLES

La Caponata Siciliana

> 500g firm aubergines
>
> 500g potatoes
>
> 1 large green pepper
>
> 1 large onion
>
> 500g firm, ripe tomatoes
>
> 200ml Italian extra-virgin olive oil
>
> 50ml white wine vinegar
>
> 2tsp sugar
>
> 2tsp salt
>
> 100g breadcrumbs

1. Peel the potatoes and the onion
2. Slit the pepper and remove any pith and pips and then cut into pieces of about 2cm
3. Dice the onion, potatoes, aubergines and tomatoes into pieces of about 2cm
4. Heat the oil in a large frying pan
5. Fry the aubergines for about 15–20 minutes, stirring frequently, until they start to brown
6. Remove with a slotted spoon and drain on absorbent paper
7. Fry the potatoes in the same way, again draining them on absorbent paper
8. Repeat the process for the onions and the peppers
9. Fry the tomatoes for about 5 minutes and drain
10. In a large bowl, combine all the fried vegetables and add the vinegar, sugar and salt and mix well

11. Fry the breadcrumbs in the remaining oil for about 5 minutes and then toss onto the vegetable mixture

12. Transfer to a serving dish

13. Leave aside for a few minutes before serving

This is also excellent eaten cold.

SOUR-SWEET ONIONS

Cipolle in Agrodolce

500g small flat onions

50ml corn oil

2tsp sugar

50ml white wine vinegar

2tsp salt

---

1. Peel the onions
2. In a large frying pan, fry the onions whole in the oil for a few minutes, turning once
3. Add the sugar, salt and vinegar
4. Reduce the heat and cover the pan with a lid
5. Allow to simmer very gently for about half an hour, turning occasionally
6. When the onions are cooked, remove the lid and fry on a high heat for a few minutes, until there is very little liquid left
7. Allow to cool before serving

STEWED ARTICHOKES

Carciofi Stufati

---

12 globe artichokes, with part of the stalk still attached

12 garlic cloves

100g fresh flat-leaf parsley

Approx. 200ml Italian extra-virgin olive oil

2tsp salt

---

1. Cut the stalks off the artichoke heads, peel and dice finely
2. Peel and finely chop the garlic
3. Pick the parsley leaves off the stalks and wash well, then finely chop
4. Place the diced artichoke stalks, garlic, parsley and salt into a bowl and thoroughly mix
5. Open up each artichoke head by bashing hard and then wash well
6. Stuff an equal amount of the parsley mixture into each artichoke head
7. In a very large heavy-bottomed saucepan or a large roasting tin, place the artichokes so that they are all standing upright
8. Put about 1tsp olive oil into each artichoke head
9. Put enough water in the saucepan to half-cover the artichokes
10. Cover with a lid or aluminium foil and cook on the stovetop for about 2 hours, checking that the water does not evaporate completely and topping up if necessary
11. Check if the artichokes are cooked by pulling off one of the inner leaves; if it comes away easily, it is ready
12. Uncover the saucepan and allow to boil for a few more minutes to reduce some of the water
13. Allow to cool a little then transfer to a serving dish where each diner will pick off the leaves and chew off the tender part of the ends

Artichokes can be found in abundance in Italy, especially during the winter and early spring. They are considered 'poor-man's meat'!

They are quite messy to eat, so be sure to provide plenty of serviettes!

STEWED CABBAGE AND POTATOES

Verza e Patate

> 1 large cabbage
>
> 500g potatoes
>
> 3 garlic cloves
>
> 50ml Italian extra-virgin olive oil
>
> 2–3tsp salt

1. Cut the leaves off the thick stalk at the base of the cabbage and wash the leaves well, then cut roughly
2. Peel and slit the garlic cloves lengthways, leaving them whole
3. In a very large heavy-bottomed saucepan, soften the garlic cloves in the oil for a few minutes without browning
4. Add the cabbage leaves and fry for a few minutes, stirring frequently
5. Pour 300ml water into the pan and add 2tsp salt
6. Cover and boil the cabbage gently for about 1 hour
7. Remove and discard the garlic cloves
8. Peel and cut the potatoes into even-sized pieces
9. Add the potatoes to the cabbage and continue cooking for about another 30 minutes, stirring frequently, until the potatoes are soft
10. Taste for salt and add more if necessary
11. Serve piping hot, together with fresh bread

STEWED MARROW

Zucca di Montagna Trifolata

1kg large marrow

1 large onion

50ml olive oil (not extra-virgin)

1 sprig fresh rosemary

2–3tsp salt

---

1. Wash the marrow well and cut into chunks of about 2cm
2. Peel and finely slice the onion
3. Detach the rosemary needles from the branch and chop
4. In a very large heavy-bottomed frying pan, soften the sliced onion in the oil for a few minutes without browning
5. Add the chunks of marrow and 2tsp salt
6. Fry for a few minutes over a high heat, stirring frequently
7. Lower the heat and add the chopped rosemary
8. Allow to cook for about 1 hour, stirring frequently, until there is very little water left
9. Raise the heat and fry the marrow until it just begins to brown
10. Serve immediately, adding salt to taste

STEWED ONIONS

Stufato di Cipolle

1kg large flat white onions

2tsp concentrated tomato paste

50ml corn oil

200ml white wine

3 leaves fresh sage

1–2tsp salt

---

1. Peel the onions and leave whole
2. In a large, heavy-bottomed frying pan, gently soften the onions in the oil for a few minutes
3. As they begin to brown, turn them over and fry on the other side
4. Stir in the wine, sage leaves and salt and allow to cook through
5. Dissolve the tomato paste in a little cold water and add this to the onions
6. Add about 100ml water and cover with a tight-fitting lid
7. Allow to cook over a very gentle heat for about 1 hour, until the onions are soft
8. Serve immediately accompanied by fresh bread

This is a very old peasant dish, from Northern Italy.

STEWED PEPPERS

Peperonata

---

1 large red pepper

1 large green pepper

1 large yellow pepper

1 large onion

1 400g tin chopped tomatoes

100ml Italian extra-virgin olive oil

1tsp salt

Freshly ground black pepper to taste

---

1. Wash the peppers well, slit and remove the stalk and all the pith and pips from the inside

2. Slice into inch-thick strips

3. Peel and finely slice the onion

4. In a large heavy-bottomed saucepan, soften the onion in the oil for a few minutes without browning

5. Add the peppers and fry on a high heat for about 5 minutes, stirring frequently

6. Add the tomatoes, salt and a dash of freshly ground black pepper

7. Stir well and lower the heat to a simmer

8. Allow to cook for about 1 hour, stirring occasionally, until the peppers are soft

9. Check for seasoning

10. Serve either hot or cold with fresh crusty bread

TINTED CAULIFLOWER

Cavolfiore Macchiato

---

1 large cauliflower

2tsp concentrated tomato paste

2 garlic cloves

25ml Italian extra-virgin olive oil

1tsp salt

---

1. Cut the cauliflower up into florets and wash well

2. In a small tea cup, dissolve the concentrated tomato paste in a little water

3. Peel and slit the garlic cloves lengthways, leaving them whole

4. In a very large heavy-bottomed saucepan, fry the garlic in the oil for a few minutes

5. Add the cauliflower florets and fry for a few minutes, stirring frequently

6. Add about 100ml water, along with the tomato mixture and salt

7. Stir well and cover with a tight-fitting lid

8. Reduce the heat and cook through very gently for about 1 hour, stirring occasionally. The cauliflower should be just underdone, but not hard

9. Before serving, add salt to taste and remove the garlic cloves

WHITE BEAN STEW

Fagioli all'Uccelletto

400g dried white Italian cannellini beans

1 400g can peeled tomatoes

4 garlic cloves

25ml Italian extra-virgin olive oil

5 leaves fresh sage

2tsp salt

Black pepper to taste

---

1. Soak the beans in cold water overnight, then boil the beans in about 2lt unsalted water for about 2 hours

2. Peel and slit the garlic cloves lengthways, leaving them whole

3. In a large heavy-bottomed saucepan, soften the garlic cloves and the sage leaves in the olive oil for a few minutes without browning

4. Drain the beans and add these to the saucepan with salt and fry for a few minutes, stirring frequently

5. Add the tomatoes and 200ml water and stir well

6. Lower the heat and allow to cook gently for about 40 minutes, stirring occasionally

7. Hunt out the garlic cloves (remember there were 4!) and discard

8. Serve immediately with crusty fresh bread and a dash of black pepper

SALADS

FENNEL SALAD

Finocchi Conditi

1kg fennel bulbs

1 lemon

30ml Italian extra-virgin olive oil

1tsp salt

---

1. Trim the fennel bulbs, leaving only the central bulb, wash well and then quarter
2. Toss in a bowl with salt and oil
3. Squeeze the lemon and filter out any pips
4. Add the lemon juice to the fennel and mix well
5. Leave aside for about 1 hour

Serve as a 'digestive' after dinner.

INVIGORATING SALAD

Insalata di Rinforzo

> 1 cauliflower
>
> 50g stoned green olives
>
> 50g stoned black olives
>
> 50g small pickled gherkins
>
> 1 piece pickled red pepper
>
> 1tsp pickled capers
>
> 100ml Italian extra-virgin olive oil
>
> 20ml white wine vinegar
>
> 1–2tsp salt

1. Wash the cauliflower well
2. Add 1tsp salt to 2lt water and bring to the boil; add the cauliflower and cook for about 15 minutes
3. Drain well and allow to cool completely
4. Break the cauliflower up into small florets and place in a large salad bowl
5. Finely dice the piece of pickled red pepper
6. Combine the olives, gherkins, capers and chopped pepper with the cauliflower
7. Add the olive oil, the vinegar and a pinch of salt and toss
8. Leave aside for about two hours before serving

This is a traditional 'must' for Neapolitans on New Year's Eve!

ONION SALAD

Insalata di Cipolle

---

3 large purple onions

1 400g can Italian borlotti beans

50ml Italian extra-virgin olive oil

20ml white wine vinegar

1tsp salt

---

1. Peel and slice the onions into very thin rings and place into a bowl full of cold water

2. Leave aside for about 2 hours

3. Drain and rinse well in fresh cold water

4. Drain the beans and rinse in cold water and drain again

5. Put the washed onion into a large bowl, together with the beans, vinegar, oil and salt and mix well

6. Leave aside for at least 1 hour before serving

SWEETS

ALMOND AND WALNUT MINI CAKES

Cavallucci

200g plain flour

100g sugar

100g ground almonds

100g chopped walnuts

50g chopped candied orange peel

½tsp ground mixed spice including: coriander, cinnamon, caraway, cloves, nutmeg, star aniseed

1tsp baking powder

50g icing sugar

Corn oil for greasing

Extra flour for dusting

---

1. Put all the dry ingredients (except the icing sugar) into a large bowl and mix well
2. Gradually add cold water until you have a smooth dough
3. With your hands well floured, form balls about the size of a mandarin
4. Lightly oil a large flat baking tray
5. Arrange the balls on the tray and flatten slightly in the centre with your thumb
6. Bake in a moderate oven for about 30–40 minutes
7. When cold, dust liberally with icing sugar and serve

These are typical at Christmas time in Tuscany.

APPLE BAKE

Pasticcio di Mele al Forno

---

4 large renette or bramley apples

250g day-old white bread

125g sultanas

1tsp ground cinnamon

Approx. 100g sugar

200ml white wine

100ml grappa

50g fine breadcrumbs

Margarine for greasing

---

1. Grease a large oven dish with a little margarine and coat with the breadcrumbs

2. Slice the bread and remove the crusts

3. Soak the slices of bread, along with the sultanas and 4tsp sugar in the white wine

4. In the meantime, peel, core and thickly slice the apples

5. Line the base of the oven dish with a layer of the now marinated bread and sultanas

6. Cover this with a layer of sliced apple, and sprinkle with a little cinnamon and about 2tsp sugar

7. Cover this with another layer of wine-soaked bread and sultanas, sliced apple and again sprinkle with sugar and cinnamon

8. Continue making layers alternating between the apples and soaked bread until they are all used up

9. Mix the grappa with whatever remains of the wine and pour over the top layer

10. Bake in a hot oven for about 40 minutes
11. Serve either hot or cold

BAKED PEACHES

Pesche al Forno

---

8 fresh firm peaches

100g ground almonds

100g chopped hazelnuts

50g fine breadcrumbs

100ml Amaretto di Saronno liqueur

100g sugar

---

1. Wash the peaches and cut in half

2. Remove the stones and discard

3. Scoop out a little of the pulp, chop and place in a mixing bowl

4. Put the peach halves into a baking tray, cut side up

5. Add the chopped hazelnuts, ground almonds, breadcrumbs, liqueur and sugar to the pulp in the bowl and mix well

6. Spoon a little of the mixture into each of the peach halves

7. Place in a moderate oven for about 40–50 minutes until they begin to caramelise

8. Allow to cool before serving

CARAMELISED ORANGES

Arance Caramellate

> *8 large oranges*
>
> *200g sugar*
>
> *6tsp Maraschino cherry liqueur*

1. Wash and peel the oranges, ensuring no pith remains; do not discard the peel

2. Using a very sharp knife, separate each segment of orange from the pithy core and place in a round on a serving platter

3. Cut the outside rind of the peel into very fine strips, discarding any of the internal white pith

4. Put the shredded orange peel into a small saucepan together with the sugar and 150ml water

5. Cook the peel very gently for about 30 minutes, stirring occasionally, until a thick syrup forms

6. Allow to cool a little and add the Maraschino liqueur

7. Spoon the caramelised peels onto the orange segments and allow to cool completely

8. Place the oranges in the fridge for at least 1 hour and serve

CHESTNUT ROUND

Castagnaccio

300g chestnut flour

50g sultanas

50g pine nuts

Corn oil for greasing

---

1. Sieve the flour into a large mixing bowl
2. Gradually add cold water until you get a lax batter
3. Brush a flat round baking tray (approx. 30cm in diameter) with some corn oil
4. Pour the chestnut batter onto the tray and scatter the sultanas and pine nuts evenly over the surface
5. Bake in moderate oven for about 30 minutes
6. Allow to cool completely before cutting into small slices to serve

A truly ancient peasant dish – you either love it or hate it!

CHRISTMAS CHOCOLATE DIAMONDS

Mustacciuoli

150g plain flour

400g icing sugar

1tsp baking powder

1tsp mixed spice including: coriander, cinnamon,
caraway, cloves, nutmeg, star aniseed

Vanilla essence

70g cocoa powder

10ml glucose syrup

30g apricot jam

Oil for greasing

Extra flour for dusting

1. Combine the flour, 100g of the sugar, baking powder and ground spices in a large bowl
2. Very gradually, add a few drops of vanilla essence and a little cold water, incorporating them until you have a compact, smooth pastry
3. Leave aside for 15 minutes
4. Roll out the pastry onto a well-floured surface to a thickness of 1cm
5. Cut out rhombus-shaped *mustacciuoli*, about 10cm by 7cm
6. Use up all the pastry scraps by re-rolling out and continue making *mustacciuoli* until you have used it all up
7. Lightly grease a large baking tray
8. Arrange the *mustacciuoli* onto the baking tray and bake in a moderate oven for 5 minutes
9. Remove the tray and turn over each piece with a spatula

10. Return the tray to the oven and bake on the other side for another 5 minutes

11. Place them on a cooling rack

12. In a small saucepan, heat the apricot jam with 1tsp icing sugar and a cup of water for about 5 minutes

13. Brush the top surface of each *mustacciuolo* with the jam

14. When these have cooled completely, turn them over and brush the other side

15. In another saucepan, gently heat the remaining icing sugar, cocoa powder, glucose syrup and 1tsp water until it begins to liquefy

16. Put the *mustacciuoli* on a large surface, preferably one that can be wiped down easily afterwards

17. Pour the chocolate glacé over one side of each of the diamonds (this is very messy!) and allow to cool completely

18. When they are completely cold, turn each one over and pour the chocolate over the other side – note: you may need to reheat the chocolate glacé

19. When they are completely cold, store in an air-tight container and serve the next day

These are a 'must' at Christmas time in the Campania region of Southern Italy.

CHRISTMAS PIE

Spongata

500g ice-cold margarine

500g plain flour

1tsp baking powder

200g apricot jam

150g sultanas

150g sugar

200g mixed chopped nuts (hazelnuts, walnuts, almonds)

100g pine nuts

1 orange

Vanilla essence

100ml anisette (aniseed liqueur)

100g icing sugar

A pinch of salt

Flour for dusting

1. Rub 300g margarine into the flour until it resembles crumbs
2. Fold in the salt and baking powder
3. Slowly add ice-cold water until you have a firm dough
4. Put in the fridge for at least 30 minutes
5. Wash the orange and grate the rind
6. In a saucepan, gently heat 200g margarine along with the jam, sugar and a little vanilla essence, stirring continuously
7. Remove from the heat and add the sultanas, chopped nuts, grated orange peel and pine nuts and mix well then leave aside to cool

8. Grease a 30cm pie dish

9. Roll out half the pastry to a 40cm round and line the pie dish

10. Mix the anisette with the fruit mixture, then pour into the pastry case

11. Roll out a second pastry round large enough to cover the pie, then seal at the edges and prick the top of the pie all over with a fork

12. Bake in a moderate oven for about 1 hour or until the pasty is golden in colour

13. Allow to cool completely, then dust generously with icing sugar

This pie keeps for several weeks if stored in a cool, dry place.

If served at Christmas time, decorate with sprigs of holly.

COFFEE ICE

Granita al Caffè

300g sugar

200ml very strong, cold black coffee

---

1. Put the sugar together with 1lt water into a saucepan and boil for about 3 minutes

2. Allow to cool completely, then stir in the coffee

3. Transfer to a bowl and place in the freezer

4. After about two hours, give the mixture a good stir and return to the freezer

6. Give the ice a stir every two hours to ensure that it does not form into one big frozen mass, but remains granulated

7. When the mixture resembles a mass of crushed ice, it is ready

8. Transfer to serving dishes and return these to the freezer

9. Remove the dishes from the freezer about 30 minutes before serving and transfer to the fridge

It is preferable to use coffee that has been made in an Italian *moka* pot.

LATTICE JAM TART

Crostata di Marmellata

> 350g plain flour
> 175g hard margarine
> 1tsp baking powder
> 1 400g jar plum jam
> Margarine for greasing
> Flour for dusting

1. Rub the margarine into the flour as finely as possible
2. Fold in the baking powder and then slowly add small amounts of cold water until you have a smooth pastry
4. Grease and flour a round 20cm flan tray
5. Roll out half the pastry and line the tray
6. Spread the jam onto the pastry base
7. With the remaining pastry, roll out and cut strips about 25cm in length and 1cm in width
8. Arrange over the surface of the jam tart in a lattice and seal the edges
9. Bake in a moderately hot oven for about 45 minutes
10. Serve cold

This tart is very commonly found in the Emilia-Romagna region where it is eaten both at breakfast time, with some good coffee, or after a meal as a sweet course. A variation of the recipe is to use apricot jam.

LEMON ICE

Granita al Limone

```
300g sugar
6 lemons
```

1. Wash the lemons well
2. Peel off the outer yellow rind, ensuring not to include any white pith
3. Boil the peel and sugar in 750ml water for about 10 minutes until you have a thin syrup
5. Remove and discard the peel and allow the syrup to cool completely
6. Squeeze the flesh of the lemons for the juice and filter out any pips
7. Add this juice to the syrup and mix well
8. Place in the freezer for about 2 hours, then give it a stir
9. Continue mixing every 2 hours so that it does not become solid
10. When it has reached the stage where it resembles a mass of crushed ice, it is ready
11. Transfer to serving dishes and return to the freezer
12. Remove from the freezer about half an hour before serving and transfer to the fridge

LEMON STRAWBERRIES

Fragole al Limone

1kg fresh ripe strawberries

1 lemon

100g sugar

---

1. Wash and quarter the strawberries
2. Place in a large bowl and gently fold in the sugar
3. Squeeze the lemon and filter any pips
4. Add the lemon juice to the strawberries and mix well
5. Place in the fridge for about 2 hours before serving
6. Serve with all the juice and some plain biscuits

PRALINE

Scruccàn

400g sugar

200g whole shelled hazelnuts

Corn oil for greasing

---

1. Toast the nuts in a moderately hot oven for about 30 minutes, until they are slightly browned

2. Allow them to cool completely

3. Liberally brush a marble slab if you have one, or alternatively a flat worktop, with oil, so that the entire surface is covered

4. Heat the sugar in a heavy-bottomed saucepan and allow to gently caramelise

5. As soon as it turns brown, remove from the heat and mix in the nuts

6. Immediately pour the mixture over the oiled surface and allow to cool completely

7. When completely cold and hardened, remove with a spatula

8. Break up into chunks and serve

PARTY FRITTERS

Frittelle

400g plain flour

1tsp baking powder

50g sugar

1 lemon

1lt corn oil

---

1. Mix the flour and baking powder in a large mixing bowl
2. Gradually add cold water until you have a very thick batter
3. Heat the oil to very hot in a deep frying pan
4. Using a dessert spoon, drop a spoonful of the batter into the hot oil
5. Allow to cook until golden in colour
6. Remove with a slotted spoon and place on absorbent kitchen paper
7. When they are all cooked, sprinkle generously with the sugar
8. Squeeze the lemon all over the fritters
9. Serve immediately

PEARS IN RED WINE

Pere al Vino Rosso

> 300ml red wine
> 1kg small firm pears
> 3 clove buds
> 1 cinnamon stick
> 200g sugar

1. Put the wine, cinnamon stick, cloves and sugar into 300ml water and bring to the boil
2. Peel, quarter and core the pears
3. When the wine mixture is boiling, add the pears and lower the heat
4. Simmer on a low heat for about 30–40 minutes, until the pears have softened a little
5. Allow to cool completely and remove the pears with a slotted spoon
6. Serve cold

The leftover wine mixture is excellent if heated and served as *vin brulè* (burnished wine) and served with roasted chestnuts, especially on cold winter nights.

SAINT JOSEPH'S DOUGHNUTS

Zeppole di San Giuseppe

400g plain flour

1tbsp brandy

50g caster sugar

1lt corn oil

100g vanilla icing sugar

Extra flour for dusting

A pinch of salt

---

1. Put the caster sugar, brandy and a pinch of salt into 300ml water and bring to the boil in a large, heavy-bottomed saucepan, then remove from the heat

2. Quickly add the flour, mixing vigorously

3. Return to the heat and continue mixing until it leaves the side of the saucepan

4. Dust a large work surface with a little flour

5. Tip the dough onto the dusted surface and allow to cool a little

6. With your hands well dusted with flour, knead the dough until it is silky smooth and no longer sticky, then form a large ball

7. Prepare a large tray with a clean, dry tea towel dusted with flour

8. Pick off a little of the dough from the ball and with your hands, form a long cigar-shaped sausage, or *zeppola*, about 1cm thick and about 15cm long

9. Join the *zeppole* up at the ends, to form a ring, and lay out on the dusted tray

10. Continue forming the *zeppole* in this way until all the dough is used up

11. Prick the surface of each *zeppola* all over with a fork

12. Turn them over and prick again with a fork

13. Heat the corn oil in a deep frying pan

14. Fry a few at a time for about 5–7 minutes, until the holes begin to bubble

15. Remove with a slotted spoon and lay out on absorbent kitchen paper

16. When they are all cooked, dust generously with the vanilla icing sugar

17. Transfer to a serving dish and serve while still warm

These are traditionally made and served around Christmas in the Naples area. They can be found being sold by street vendors around town squares.

WINE BISCUITS

Ciambelline Campagnole

> *250g plain flour*
>
> *100g sugar*
>
> *100ml red wine*
>
> *100ml olive oil (not extra-virgin)*
>
> *Extra flour for dusting*

1. Brush a large flat baking tray with a little of the olive oil
2. Put the wine, oil and sugar in a large bowl and mix well
3. Sieve the flour into the wine mixture, stirring all the time
4. Continue adding flour until you have a smooth dough
5. Dust a large work surface with flour
6. Knead the pastry until it is silky smooth
7. Form a ball and cover with a damp tea towel, and leave aside for 1 hour
8. With well-floured hands, pick off pieces of pastry and form long cigar shapes of about 10cm in length and 1cm thick
9. Join up the ends to form a ring
10. Place each biscuit on the baking tray
11. Continue forming biscuits until all the pastry is used up
12. Bake in a moderate oven for about 30–40 minutes
13. When cold, store in an air-tight container

These are very nice together with 'Vin Santo' – a type of fortified wine – or port or sweet sherry if you cannot find Vin Santo.

PRESERVES

DRUNKEN CHERRIES

Ciliegie sotto Spirito

1kg firm ripe cherries
Approx 500ml grappa

---

1. Wash the cherries well and remove any stalks
2. Dry them thoroughly with a clean tea towel
3. Pack the cherries into clean, dry jam jars and fill with the grappa
4. Ensure that the cherries are completely immersed and that the jar is full to the brim
5. Screw the lids on as tightly as possible
6. Store in a dark place for at least three months – the longer, the better

These are very strong and wicked!

PICKLED ARTICHOKES

Carciofi sott'Olio

> *20 globe artichokes*
>
> *500ml white wine vinegar*
>
> *1 lemon*
>
> *Approx. 500ml Italian extra-virgin olive oil*
>
> *5 bay leaves*
>
> *5tsp salt*

1. Prepare a large bowl with 1lt cold water and the juice of the lemon
2. Strip the artichokes of all the outer leaves
3. Cut off the stalk and the tops of the leaves, leaving only the central heart of the artichokes
4. Cut each heart in half and remove any beard that there may be, then immediately plunge the hearts into the lemon water, to prevent them going black
5. In a large saucepan, mix the vinegar with 1lt water and bring to the boil
6. Drain the artichokes from the lemon water and add to the saucepan
7. Allow to boil for about 5 minutes
8. Prepare a tray with a clean, dry tea towel
9. Scoop the artichoke hearts out with a slotted spoon and place on the tea towel
10. Allow to dry completely for at least 3 hours (preferably overnight)
11. Fill 5 jam jars with boiling water and allow to stand
12. When the water in the jars is cold, empty and carefully dry the jars with a clean tea towel

13. Put a little olive oil together with one bay leaf and 1tsp salt into one of the jars and stir

14. Start packing in the artichoke hearts, pushing down with a fork

15. Pack as many as will nearly fill the jar and then add enough olive oil to completely cover them

16. Press down again with a fork to expel any trapped air

17. Screw the lid on as tightly as possible

18. Continue with the other jars in the same way until all the artichoke hearts have been packed

19. Store the jars in a cool dry place (not the fridge) for at least one month before serving

As a variation, instead of using bay leaf, substitute with rosemary or with chilli-pepper or garlic.

PICKLED AUBERGINES

Melanzane sott'Olio

1kg firm long aubergines

500ml white wine vinegar

Approx. 300ml Italian extra-virgin olive oil

3tsp coarse salt

2tsp salt

---

1. Peel the aubergines, and slice as thinly as possible lengthways

2. Arrange the aubergines in a colander, sprinkle with coarse salt and toss evenly, then leave, covered with a small bowl or flat plate weighted by a 1kg bag of sugar; place the colander over a bowl so that any liquid that accumulates is caught

3. Leave for at least 4 hours, preferably overnight, a fair quantity of liquid should gather in the bowl, which should then be discarded

4. Wash the aubergine slices well and lay them out onto a clean tea towel to dry

5. Pat away any excess liquid with kitchen paper

6. In a large saucepan, mix the vinegar with 1lt water and bring to the boil

7. Add the aubergine slices to the pan and boil for about 5 minutes

8. With a slotted spoon, remove the slices and again lay them out to dry on a clean tea towel and pat dry

9. Fill 2 small jam jars (or one large) with boiling water and allow to stand until the water has turned cold

10. Empty the jars and dry thoroughly with a clean tea towel

11. Pour enough olive oil into each jar to reach about a third of the way up and mix in 1tsp salt

12. Pack as many aubergine slices as possible into the jar as will fit, pressing down with a fork, then cover completely and top up to the brim with olive oil, ensuring that all of the aubergine slices are below the surface of the oil

13. Screw the tops on as tightly as possible

14. Store the jars in a cool place (not the fridge) for at least one month before opening

If preferred, garlic cloves or herbs such as rosemary, bay leaf or oregano; even chilli peppers can be added to the oil.

These are a great as reserve food, especially for a quick meal, when there is no time to cook, served with some good bread, they are delicious and hearty.

PICKLED MIXED VEGETABLES

Giardiniera

> *1 small cauliflower*
>
> *2 carrots*
>
> *2 large sticks celery*
>
> *1 red pepper*
>
> *1 yellow pepper*
>
> *100g small white onions*
>
> *200g French green beans*
>
> *1½lt white wine vinegar*
>
> *Approx. 700ml Italian extra-virgin olive oil*
>
> *6tsp salt*

1. Wash and chop the celery to pieces about 2cm in length
2. Top and tail and wash the green beans and chop to pieces of about 2cm
3. Peel the carrots and slice into thin rounds
4. Wash the cauliflower and break up into small florets, discarding the thick central stalk
5. Wash the peppers and slit open, then remove all the pith and pips
6. Slice the peppers into pieces about 2cm x 1cm
7. Peel the onions, leaving them whole
8. In a large saucepan, add 1tsp salt and the vinegar to 1lt water and bring to the boil
9. Throw in all the vegetables and allow to boil for about 15 minutes
10. Drain the vegetables well
11. Lay out all the vegetables onto clean, dry tea towels to dry out completely, preferably overnight

12. Fill five empty jam jars with boiling water and allow to stand

13. When the water in the jars has cooled completely, empty and thoroughly dry them with a clean tea towel

14. In each jar, put a little olive oil and 1tsp salt

15. Toss the vegetables in a large bowl

16. Pack the vegetables into each jar, pressing down with a fork, until they nearly reach the top

17. Fill the jars with olive oil, ensuring that all the vegetables are completely immersed

18. Screw the tops on the jars as tightly as possible

19. Leave for at least a month before serving

PICKLED YELLOW PEPPERS

Peperoni sott'Olio

1kg firm yellow peppers

750ml white wine vinegar

3tsp salt

Approx. 500ml Italian extra-virgin olive oil

2tsp dried oregano

2 garlic cloves

---

1. Wash the peppers and slit them downwards to carefully remove all the pith and pips
2. Cut the flesh into strips about 1cm thick, keeping the whole length
3. Put the vinegar into a saucepan together with 750ml water and salt
4. Bring to the boil and add the pepper slices
5. Boil rapidly for about 10 minutes
6. Drain the pepper slices and lay them out onto a clean, dry tea towel to dry completely
7. Fill two empty jam jars with boiling water and leave aside to cool
8. Peel the garlic cloves and cut into slices
9. When the water in the jars has cooled, empty and thoroughly dry the jars with a clean tea towel
10. Put a little oil, 1tsp oregano and a few pieces of garlic into each jar
11. Pack the pepper slices into the jars, pressing down with a fork, ensuring there are no air bubbles, until they almost reach the top
12. Top up with more oil, ensuring that the peppers are completely immersed
13. Screw the tops on as tightly as possible

14. Store in a cool place (not the fridge) for at least three weeks before serving

These are great as snack food, when there is no time to prepare anything.

LaVergne, TN USA
27 May 2010
184203LV00001B/69/P